THOM
TWIN

THOMPSON
TWIN

An '80s Memoir

Michael White

LITTLE, BROWN AND COMPANY

A *Little, Brown* Book

First published in Great Britain in 2000
by Little, Brown and Company

Copyright © 2000 by Michael White

The moral right of the author has been asserted.

A CIP catalogue record for this book
is available from the British Library.

ISBN: 0 316 85198 1

Typeset in Imprint by M Rules
Printed and bound in Great Britain
by Clays Ltd, St Ives plc

Little, Brown and Company (UK)
Brettenham House
Lancaster Place
London WC2E 7EN

For Tim
A friend at the beginning, a friend always.

FOREWORD

Long, long ago, in a galaxy far, far away, when the events described here had just happened, I tried to write what I felt about them, but I was far too close in time and my emotions were too raw. Standing back, two decades on, I think I can see more clearly; the details might be less well-defined, but the panorama is certainly bigger, the focus crisper.

I have called this book *Thompson Twin: An '80s Memoir* because although I was not with the band for long, I was a member of the Thompson Twins at a crucial moment in the group's career – just as the world was about to fall at their feet. But there is more to this tale than my time with the Thompson Twins. It is also the story of how pop music can trap and liberate, inspire and destroy, elevate and enervate. This is the story of how I became obsessed with music, how I found fame and success and then lost it all in an instant. It is also the story of the teenage angst that powers the chords and drives the beat of pop music but can ignite and explode when combined with love, setting to flame dreams, wishes and hopes.

As I started to write, I began to think that in many ways I am no longer the person in this tale; that Michael White has long since faded into the past, I believed. Reflecting on these times I found it hard to engage with what I once was and sometimes actually felt ashamed of what I had done, oddly repelled by the feelings I once had. But then I realised that for all the peripheral differences between my life in 1980 and that in 2000 I am still the same person I was two decades ago. I certainly feel the same way about music – I've even started playing and recording again.

In writing this I wanted to tell a story I have recounted many times to almost everyone who has got to know me, a tale upon which I have dined well. But I also wanted to re-create the mood and flavour of the time, the transition from late 1970s to early 1980s Britain, a time during which our lives went through enormous changes politically and culturally.

This period is now officially 'history'. Doesn't that make you feel old?

Michael White
London, January 2000

'The music business is run by drug addicts and shoe-salesmen.'

IAN DURY

1

This story begins with two scenes, in memory slow-mo.

In the first I'm sitting at a table in a long, narrow room in a psychiatric hospital in the South Bronx. The date is 17 November 1982. It's freezing and dark outside and the cold New York air clings to me still. Two weeks ago I was on stage with a band who are about to become one of the biggest pop acts in the world. But right now I'm waiting for a 21-year-old woman named Jan, a woman I've lived with for three years, and I have never been so scared in my entire life. My stomach is churning and I cannot stop my hands shaking. I hear telephones, the alien trill of American phones, and sirens wailing their way on to 183rd Street. From a room along the corridor, loud voices and laughter, American voices that remind me how far I am from home, how far I've come from the life I thought I knew.

The orderly who met me at reception tells me he won't be

long, he says I should prepare myself. But nothing can prepare me for the moment a few minutes later when he turns a
corner back into the long, narrow room. He is holding the
hand of a petite young woman. She is wearing a brightly
patterned dress, baggy grey socks around her ankles, no
shoes. Her hair is crimson and sprayed to stiff points that
radiate from her head. She has black eye make-up smeared
across her cheeks and her face looks hollow, as though I could
poke a finger through the papier-mâché skin. She looks at the
wall as she passes, then she turns to me. Jan eases into a chair
on the other side of the table and the orderly walks away.

At first I'm lost. As I look at Jan I feel the churning inside
turn to flames. I can see she has absolutely no idea who I am.
But I pretend everything is okay, I pretend not to notice that
she looks awful. I tell her about the flight over from London
and about the after-dark subway journey from Manhattan
and the bus ride from the station with the wide-eyed casual-
ties sitting in the back. With banality born of desperation, I
ask her what the food is like, tell her how I heard what had
happened, but she says nothing. I take out a photograph of
the flat we shared, pictures of our friends back home, snaps
from happier days. She looks at them and I kid myself a
smile flickers across her face and around her eyes, and for a
second I allow myself hope.

Then, suddenly, she screams and jumps up, knocking the
chair across the floor. The orderly returns and holds her
gently, coaxing her back to the seat. I'm standing, shaking,
tears well and then brim over on to my cheeks. I wipe my
face, trying desperately to conceal my feelings. Jan laughs,
but it is an empty, confused and humourless laugh; and when
she speaks I wish she hadn't. The words are meaningless, but
that's not the worst of it: her voice is nothing but a squeak, a
shrill broken whine that turns into an incoherent gurgle as
she grabs one of the photographs still lying on the table. She
holds it close to her eyes then flings it to the floor, does a

pirouette and wanders off to find her room beyond the corridor, beyond the veil of everyday life.

In the second scene, it is fifteen days earlier: 8 P.M. on 2 November 1982, and I'm about to hit the stage of the Hammersmith Palais, London, as keyboard player and guitarist for the Thompson Twins.

This ought to be the most exhilarating experience of my life, but in fact as I wait for the lights to come up I feel more confused and disorientated than I have ever felt during my twenty-three years on this planet. The reasons for this are, in increasing order of importance: a) no food for two days; b) no sleep for three days; c) too much cocaine; and d) Jan, the girl standing next to me as we line up at the edge of the stage.

Jan and I have been together since O-level year, we've been engaged for two years and joined the band together, but only three days have passed since I first learned that she is sleeping with John Hade, the Thompson Twins' manager. She told me at four in the morning after the band returned from a show at the Lyceum, Sheffield.

How this could have happened, and how ironic it is that it should have happened just as I reach what I think is the zenith of my life, are all I have been thinking about since leaving Sheffield on the tour bus one drizzly morning to start heading south to play the final date of the British leg of the band's first international tour. But, as the disco stops and the lights go down, an expectant hush then falls over the crowd, which begins to pack together still closer at the front of the stage. At that moment, as I walk the few yards to the keyboard plinth and stand in readiness, all thoughts stop. All feelings of betrayal and loss vanish as I watch the stage suddenly flood with light and the drummer, Boris Williams, lurches into the first song, 'Lies'. I can see no further than my own fingers, but I can hear the 3,000-strong audience erupt with a single, unified gasp as the song kicks in, pounding through the p.a. system, the sound bouncing off the walls and slamming around the cavernous auditorium.

In that moment, all pain has gone, the cold churning in the pit of my stomach has evaporated and I'm swept up in the music. The heat hits me from the audience and the beat from the stage, the bass drum thumping in my abdomen. And I'm part of this organism, I'm making a part of this sound, it swells through my fingers, I'm generating this excitement as I stab at the keys and dance around behind my Prophet V synthesiser like Joe 90 on acid.

Tom Bailey steps up to the microphone and starts to sing, and I join in with backing vocals. Bassist Andrew Bodnar, six-four and sporting a black sombrero, jumps from some steps at the back of the stage and swings his guitar as he punches the air with thick, precise bass notes. Alannah Currie bounces on the spot bashing a tambourine and Joe Leeway, his hair a mass of dreadlocks, hammers away at percussion. Jan beside me mirrors what I do, adding light keyboard flourishes to the sound and leaning into the microphone to add a harmony vocal. We are one being, a perfectly synchronised unit, thinking in unison, doing precisely what we have been rehearsing for so long.

I can see Jan as she dances and plays and sings. She looks brimming with confidence, full of life. Yet now, from the other end of the telescope, I see her on the edge of a precipice, about to topple over the edge. But how could any of us have known then what destiny had in store for her?

And, as the music fills me, I finally reach the long-awaited apotheosis, a Damascus moment, an Epstein-seeing-the-Beatles-for-the-first-time freeze-frame, a moment when nothing else matters but the music and the adulation sweeping up from all those people a few yards away. Although a part of me knows this will not last, that this supreme moment will be swamped by life's demands, by sorrow and fatigue, in spite of everything, for one delirious, orgasmic, Tantric moment, this truly is the most exhilarating experience of my life.

Nothing else matters.

2

'You look like a guitarist,' she said. And that's how it all started.

It was the summer of 1976, a year before punk went ballistic, the year Boney M appeared in the Top 10; a heat-wave summer when Bjorn Borg first won Wimbledon, the US celebrated its bicentennial and Carter stood ready to replace Ford. Jan and I and a group of school friends were sitting drinking illicitly in the Smack Inn, a pub in Old Leigh near Southend-on-Sea, Essex.

I don't know why I took Jan's remark seriously, but I did. Aged seventeen, I had shoulder-length hair, harboured a liking for flares and tatty plimsolls, longed to own an Afghan coat but couldn't afford one and had never played a musical instrument in my life. But apparently I looked like a guitarist, so that was that.

I certainly liked the idea of emulating the musicians I most admired, all of whom were guitarists – Steve Howe of Yes, Steve Hackett of Genesis and David Gilmour of Pink Floyd, but it wasn't that. I think I was just flattered by the idea that I could look like a guitarist, whatever that meant, and so I immediately began saving to buy the necessary equipment to complete the image.

I was already leading an unconventional existence for a seventeen-year-old. During my second A-level year, my parents had moved thirty miles from where I was at school and Jan's father had kindly allowed me to move into their house, where I had a tiny room on the top floor. School I hardly attended, preferring to spend my days reading Hermann Hesse novels, the odd physics textbook and listening to Emerson, Lake & Palmer albums. When I was bored with these I wrote bad poetry and made endless, fruitless attempts to begin a novel in the German Expressionist style.

The guitar I finally managed to purchase cost £10 and came from a junk shop on a street running parallel to Southend East railway station. Like all instruments, any guitar worth its name should possess certain virtues. It should have a straight, carefully crafted neck, good fretting and most importantly for the aspiring rock musician, it should have what's called 'good action'. This means the strings should lay at precisely the right distance from the fretboard (the part upon which you place fingers of the left hand – if you're right-handed – to position notes and chords). A good action makes a guitar much easier to play, and to learn on. My first guitar, quickly christened 'the railway sleeper', had no virtues whatsoever. In fact, it was an anti-guitar – it had a warped neck, bad fretting, atrocious action – with the strings standing at least a quarter of an inch too far from the neck. In short, it was a miracle I got anything out of it at all. And some would argue I didn't.

Jan and I formed our first band a few weeks after the conversation in the Smack Inn. After enormous deliberation

(typical of all aspiring rock bands) we named ourselves
Mother Earth. That's right: one year before punk, we
formed a band called Mother fucking Earth. The band was a
three-piece, emulating, I believe, Emerson, Lake & Palmer.
Jan and I were complemented by a drummer called Dave
Humphreys. Jan sang and played flute and I did my best to
sound like Steve Howe joining ELP for a special set. When
we weren't playing flutes, drums or guitars, we all had a stab
at percussion, sometimes all together. After a few sessions, we
recorded a tape in Dave's parents' living room, sellotaping a
microphone from a tiny mono cassette player to a chair-back.
The first person we played it to said we sounded like someone dancing in chain-mail.

Young musicians in their first bands seem to have some
sort of self-protecting immunity to criticism. It is said that
women have a number of particular chemicals in the brain
which make them forget the pain of childbirth so they can
contemplate pregnancy a second time. I think musicians have
a similar brain chemical. It makes us deaf to our own cre-
ations, surrounds whatever we do in those early days with the
smell of roses. Hemingway once said that all good writers
must have an in-built bullshit-detector, but young musicians
cannot afford such luxury, at least not until they are able to
play and write. I have no doubt that if I could hear what
Dave, Jan and I did then with today's ears I would have
burned that piece of wood masquerading as a guitar there
and then and never, ever have recorded another thing in my
life. But no, we went on, recorded more utterly appalling
tapes and even (and God, my buttocks hurt with clenching so
hard at the memory) played live, unarmed with anything
approaching musicality.

It was a year after our first tentative efforts in Dave's parents' front room. By this time Dave and his long-suffering
family had moved to Sussex, which had brought an abrupt
stop to Jan and I turning up on their doorstep each Saturday

with flutes, guitars and assorted percussion. It was the summer before I was due to leave for university, hot and inspiring, the Jubilee year when Elvis fell off the toilet, Boycott reached a hundred centuries and *Star Wars* burst into our consciousness.

Along the way we had acquired a new drummer (another friend from school) and a keyboard player called Christine. I say she was a 'keyboard player' but really she was no more competent than us, and rather than emulating Keith Emerson and his bank of synthesisers, Christine was the proud owner of a Bontempi organ which had come from a catalogue, and an ersatz keyboard from Australia called a stylophone, which must qualify as the worst thing to come out of that fair country.

The concert was in the local hall, in which the Darby and Joan club met each afternoon and Southend East mothers' coffee mornings were held three times a week. The stage was a cliché, a school play affair, which in a way was singularly appropriate because the entire event possessed a similar atmosphere – the infants' Christmas nativity.

We had a pair of spotlights, which were actually a set of late '60s ceiling lights found in Christine's parents' garage. These we screwed to a plank of wood, replacing the bulbs with one green and one red spot. The whole contraption was then positioned at the front of the stage, pointing our way. We had no form of p.a. system, so Jan's vocals were amplified through a spare guitar amp I had borrowed from yet another school friend. Christine shared my amp and we just balanced the volumes on the instruments. The rest of the sound was provided by the drummer (thankfully unamplified) and the ubiquitous percussion.

We rehearsed intensively for the big gig and sold tickets to our families and friends, knowing that if it all went terribly wrong we'd be leaving for university in a few weeks so it didn't really matter. We prepared our stage clothes with

meticulous care. I wore, I recall, a pair of flares and a baggy,
billowy-sleeved pseudo-medieval top made from faux silk.
Jan had run it up on her pedal-powered sewing machine and
it was modelled on a shirt Jon Anderson of Yes had worn in
a photo accompanying an *NME* article I had read and re-
read many, many times that summer . . . the summer of
'Anarchy In The UK'.

Before hitting the stage I was as nervous as I had ever
been, but I knew this was an important day. I knew this was
the first serious stepping-stone to superstardom, an essential
preparation for the 'real thing'.

I can't say I remember a single song we played, but in any
event, 'song' is probably an inappropriate word for the material we were writing and performing as Mother Earth. Like
our heroes, we went in for ten- or even twenty-minute
'pieces', compositions that had 'movements' and were based
upon 'meaningful concepts', just like the side-long 'movements' of the concept albums we bought and cherished and
played until they were worn through by the stylus.

The problem was that bands that made concept albums
could *play*, they had huge followings and they sold millions
of records and even then they were considered horribly pretentious and were (in most cases, quite rightly) mauled by the
critics. Sadly, Mother Earth shared with these bands none of
their qualities save the last. I cannot begin to imagine the
horror of embarrassment and sheer tedium we subjected our
thirty-strong audience to that hideous afternoon, and even
now I cannot believe how patient they were to remain seated
and straight-faced throughout.

To be fair to ourselves, we did try. We may have been
incompetent, but however misguided we were from first
notion to final execution of our music, we did believe in what
we were doing. Perhaps it was because of this that I personally felt hurt by the swingeing reviews. When I say reviews I
mean rather the one comment I knew was said with honesty

and came from an impartial member of the audience, a friend of one of my school friends. He said our performance should have been treated like masturbation – done quietly, and in private.

3

When I first met Jan, her mother was dying of cancer. The family lived in a draughty Victorian terrace in one of the less salubrious streets in town, a turning off York Road in Southend East, an area once favoured by prostitutes and sailors. After ill health had forced early retirement from his job as a coalman, Jan's father worked as a part-time petrol-station attendant. Her mother had been a plump, ruddy-cheeked and jolly woman, and had done her best to remain in good spirits even when she was suffering daily agony. Jan's mother had gone into service at the age of thirteen and could only marvel at the fact that, as she lay dying, her youngest daughter was heading for university. Often after rehearsals in the front room of their home or returning from Dave's parents, I would sit up late talking to Jan's mum. She had had no education to speak of, but she was wise and knowing. She once stared at me in disbelief when I told her that the earth moved through space and orbited the sun, a star like any other; but a moment later she would offer some gem of advice I only appreciated years later. When she died in 1976, a hollowness took over the house, and that winter felt especially chill.

Jan and I had met during a school holiday when I was fifteen. Our first date was spent babysitting for her older brother, Fred, and his wife. Considering our ages, our relationship was unusually intense from the start, and today I have mixed feelings about the seven years we spent together, through O-levels, A-levels and university. On the one hand, I know this was a period during which I should have had a long string of girlfriends, but on the other, I think I learned a great deal by being with one person for so long at such a tender age. It just meant that after we separated I was sowing wild oats as my friends were settling down with their first wives.

Our backgrounds were very similar. My mother had gone into service for a surgeon and his family in East London when she was only fourteen. My father had been more successful than Jan's; after the Second World War he had set up his own business, and by the 1960s, for a short time at least, he owned a string of shops selling kitchens and bathrooms. But Jan's father was a gentle, morose soul, devoid of all ambition whose one love (aside from his family) was his garden, which he tended with devotion and patience, transforming what would have been a drab urban backyard into a riot of scent and colour. By contrast, my father, who had his shy and reserved moments, was on the whole more outward-looking and energetic. But to recall his directionless ambition is probably my most painful childhood memory. The problem could be summed up in one word: gee-gees. Dad was a compulsive gambler whose habit drove the family into bankruptcy and beyond. Whereas Jan lived her entire childhood and teenage years in a rented but reliable home, I spent spells

of unpredictable length in luxurious houses and the worst
slums, depending upon the state of my father's business and
his luck on the horses.

We moved house so frequently during my childhood that
by the age of eleven I had lost track of our various ex-
addresses and the different schools I had attended. The
reason my parents had moved away in 1976 leaving me in
Southend was because my father's fortunes had hit an all-
time low. The last place we all shared as a family (my parents,
my younger sister and myself) was a two-bedroomed flat over
a closed-up shop my father had found through a gambling
buddy. What Dad's friend hadn't told him was that the place
was about to be condemned and had rats in the yard. The
final three months there were hell; first the electricity, then
the gas, then the water were disconnected because the bills
had not been paid. Needless to say, my father was picking the
wrong nags.

For much of that time I was staying over at Jan's house
anyway, returning every few days to discover new horrors:
cockroaches in the bathroom, more holes in the ceiling, more
amenities disconnected, pieces of furniture missing, only to
be spotted later in the local pawn-shop. By this time, my
father was beyond help, floundering in a depression that
had all but paralysed him and pushed my mother and my
fourteen-year-old sister to the very edge of despair. It
seemed as though no one could help until one of my elder
sisters somehow succeeded in finding my parents and sister
a council house in a new development in Braintree, some
thirty miles away.

I think it was this background of shared but very different
hopelessness that had first brought Jan and I together, and
then music had gelled us, transforming what would probably
have been a short-lived teenage thing into a long-lasting and
often claustrophobically intense relationship. But I had been
contaminated by my father's over-ambition and Jan had

inherited the laid-back personality of her father. From the beginning I drove us on, I was the one desperate to succeed. At first, Jan knew far more about music than me and she had a great voice; I was starting completely from scratch, but really I have my father to thank for a career that led Jan and me from a church hall and a stage with two spotlights to a US tour, hit records and beyond. And perhaps that's where the self-protective immunity to criticism comes from. Maybe it originates from the same place as the hunger to succeed at all costs, from the fact we had nothing to lose.

4

And so the unhipness continued. While busily working on our twenty-minute opuses, Jan and I hit upon the idea of earning a little money playing covers in wine bars and clubs. By this time I had a cheap acoustic guitar, which for covers of songs like 'If You're Going To San Francisco' and 'Blowin' In The Wind' was far more appropriate than my old railway sleeper.

This was spring 1978. Our lives had changed enormously during the preceding nine months. We were both now at university in London; Jan at Goldsmith's College in New Cross and I was at King's on the Strand. We both had grants and had both taken advantage of a loophole in the grant system which meant that we actually made money from a travel allowance awarded to students living more than forty miles from their college. We found a basement flat in Old Leigh, on an elegant, tree-lined street called Grand Parade, a short walk from the railway station on the Fenchurch Street line which took us almost directly to both colleges, with only a short tube ride at the other end.

The beginning of college life felt precisely the right time to break away from Jan's father's house and to begin living together. Life had grown uncomfortable in the freezing house in Southend and the prospect of another winter in my tiny room at the top held little attraction. Apart from this, one afternoon a few weeks before term was due to begin, Mr C. had walked in on Jan and I in a position upon her bed most fathers would not care to witness. Nothing had been said, but from that moment on, the atmosphere at supper had been as thick as treacle, and both Jan and I were soon desperate to get out.

The flat was tiny, just two rooms in a huge house over-looking the sea. Unfortunately it was in the basement, so the sea view was a little obscured, but renting the flat was nevertheless by far the most hip thing we had ever done in our lives and the place soon became a magnet for all the people we were beginning to meet on the Essex music scene. The only trouble was that at £20 a week it was expensive: hence the need to play the wine-bar circuit.

But it was torture. We were paid £10 by the more generous venues, and £7 by the others; and this for two sets of at least one hour each through a weekend lunchtime or midweek evening, playing to a ragtag collection of drinkers who showed no interest in what we were doing. The worse part was lugging the equipment to and from the bars. Even as a two-piece folk unit we needed a guitar, a mic, a stand and an amplifier for Jan's voice. We caught a bus from Old Leigh to Southend (where all the venues were) and the walk from the bus-stop to the club was arm-wrenching and exhausting. But then, this is the lot of many a jobbing musician, and skilled players go through this routine day after day, night after night for a lifetime. We could hardly complain.

On the other hand, there were rewards from playing to inebriated businessmen letching over Jan and to families out for Sunday lunch. Most importantly we developed enormously as musicians. It took weeks to learn twenty or thirty classic songs for the two sets, and it took discipline and guts to get up and perform in such an environment week after week with no audience appreciation. Jan had a good voice, and by this time I was improving as a musician; I had mastered the half-dozen chords needed to play almost any pop song and I could make a half-decent impersonation of a professional musician. Problems only started when we decided to introduce a few of our own numbers into the set.

Suddenly we went from being almost invisible to being labelled by the management as weirdos. First the Sunday gigs went and then the evenings slipped away. There were no explanations, just a 'thanks for playing here for a while, but we thought we'd try something different from next week. Here's an extra two quid.' By the time we realised the problem, it was too late.

It wasn't as if we were attempting two-piece versions of one of the 'concept' tracks, nor even the shortened fifteen-minute version of 'Galadriel's Hair' – we were just incorporating a couple of what we thought were 'pop songs'.

Despite only holding down these gigs for a few months, we saved a little money from the venture and, ignoring the feelings of Southend wine-bar managers, we decided to make a proper recording of some of our songs, with the distant, embryonic thought that we might try to approach a record company with the results. Yes, that good old immunity to criticism *thang* was still alive and well and had many, many years of wear left in it still.

By this time we had met a few musicians, some of whom shared our slightly odd approach to pop, and others who didn't but were game for anything. Tim Alexander was only sixteen when we met him playing in a band called Fragment, and, as nineteen-year-olds with our own flat, we became almost surrogate mother and father to him for a while. A year earlier his parents had moved to Devon to follow his father's job, leaving Tim to finish school in Southend. Tim lived near us in his grandparents' one-bedroomed flat. He made a bed each night in the bath and was awakened each morning by the uncomely odours and sounds of his grandfather's bowel movements in the toilet the other side of a stud wall.

Tim had (and still has) the stamp of genius upon him, and I realised this the moment I saw him playing in Southend High Street one Saturday with the rest of his band. To me they were highly accomplished musicians but were somehow stuck in the rut of playing Genesis covers, while their own songs also sounded, well . . . just like Genesis covers. Such criticism was of course terribly hypocritical of me, as Tim so endearingly pointed out about six seconds after listening to some of my own stuff. I wasn't doing Genesis covers, just covering all angles of progressive rock – badly. At least Fragment could play.

Tim more or less moved into our flat, only returning very late most nights to the bath at his grandparents' around the corner. Neither Jan nor I got on at all well with the other two members of Fragment, a guitarist of great talent called Jono and the gifted but conventional-sounding drummer/vocalist, Dave. I think I harboured a certain jealousy for Jono's musical skill and there was a distinct competitiveness between Dave and Jan that soured our relationship. Amazingly, the band are still together as the original three-piece, and are now one of the most successful groups in Holland.

Tim is a brilliant all-round musician, who plays guitar, drums, synth and piano all superbly well. He introduced us to another Tim, Tim Plater, who was an even better pianist. With a square, chiselled jaw that gave him an air of

Desperate Dan, Tim Plater looked suitably eccentric, but his rather slow, plodding manner often made him difficult to work with. He had quite different musical tastes and completely different aspirations from us. Whereas I viewed music as a surrogate religion (and still do), Tim saw it as a meal ticket. And indeed he would go on to play in a succession of cabaret acts and club bands, and one night, a decade or more after we parted company, I'm sure I spotted him on *Top of the Pops* playing keyboards for some faceless band whose name has melted into the past. He looked exactly the same, a gentle ivory-tickler straight out of the *Beano*.

To fill out the sound, we decided to try to find a second guitarist, someone to add acoustic guitar to my lead, and Jan found a suspiciously good-looking young guy named Paul Webb, whom she had been introduced to by an old school friend who lived across the road from Paul and had seen him leaving his parents' house with a guitar case. This of course was insufficient qualification, even for us, but inspired I imagine by his good looks, Jan had invited him over to the flat to see what he was made of. He turned out to be a bassist in a local band, but was actually another horribly talented all-rounder like Tim. He seemed a nice bloke and Jan was very persuasive, so then we were five.

The two Tims and Paul worked well together as we pieced together a makeshift band to get the recording done. We all rehearsed in Tim Plater's parents' home for a short while, a house close to Jan's father's. On winter evenings I swear it was colder inside than out. There were times we tried to play our instruments wearing gloves. These rehearsals were often fraught affairs with all of us pulling in different directions, but after much deliberation we managed to select four songs which were pared down to what we considered 'song' length. The most important to us was an instrumental we called 'Angrenost'. I'm ashamed to say that this title came from an episode in *The Lord of the Rings*;

something to do with the winter home of the evil wizard. The music had nothing to do with the book and the connection was simply a pretension I can only now admit to. It was however quite a stirring little ditty, and we saw it as our best chance with a record company, reasoning that there must be someone out there who wanted to go against the grain and do something different from the Sex Pistols or The Clash. The other songs were 'If The War Goes On', a bit of a rocker, I recall, with a thrusting guitar solo; 'Already', a jazzy little number with a cool breezy feel played on acoustic guitar, and 'Optimum Population', a song that sounded like a dissertation from a sociology course but was actually a rather meaningless diatribe about the evils of over-populating the earth. Really.

The Tims were doing it for the experience. Although musically they were streets ahead of Jan or me, like us, neither of them had been in a proper recording studio before. I don't really know why Paul had agreed to be part of the band, but actually, after three or four rehearsals he no longer was. One day I bumped into him in town the morning after he had missed a rehearsal and he told me that all along he had been rehearsing three days a week in London with another group. They were called Talk Talk, he said, and I remember laughing in his face when he informed me they were about to sign to EMI. I never saw Paul again, apart from when he appeared with Talk Talk on *Top of the Pops*.

The line-up was completed by a crazy drummer called Neil Sharp. I had known Neil vaguely at school, but then everyone in the school knew Neil vaguely. He was seen as a disaster on legs, and I had spent the two years of sixth form studiously avoiding him.

That aside, he was supposed to be a great drummer. But in fact, he wasn't. Barely able to keep time, he would fly off at musical tangents and try to dominate the sound we were attempting to create. Musically, he was the very last thing we needed, but he had a car, so all was forgiven.

And actually, Neil turned out to be great fun. His motto was: 'There is nothing so overrated as a bad fuck and nothing so underrated as a good shit.' In his own odd way he made an important difference to what we were trying to do and added a bit of cred to our tedious, post-hippie seriousness. He even offered us a song, '10,000 Babies', which went: 'Baby, baby, baby, baby, baby, baby, baby, baby . . .'

Because he was working (as an insurance clerk), to us, Neil seemed unimaginably rich. He had the best drum kit you could wish for, he had an amazing camera with a set of lenses and he seemed to know everyone on the local music scene, from sound engineers to lighting men who had been on tour with the Rolling Stones. He also had a friend who worked at a better studio than the one we had booked, and he managed to persuade us to cancel and rebook there.

The new studio was in London. We hadn't planned for that, but the two Tims became very excited at the prospect of recording in London and our anxieties over the cost of getting our gear to said studio were soon allayed when our three band members agreed to chip in for the cost of a van. Furthermore, we had Neil's assurance that the London studio was an eight-track instead of the four-track in Southend, and his pal was charging less. How could we refuse?

To say our first sight of a real studio in London, with a London-based sound man and a Cockney engineer was a disappointment would be something of an understatement. It was in a basement of a tenement in the East End and comprised two rooms reached by descending a narrow and very steep staircase, which was frightening to negotiate with the obligatory selection of bulky musical equipment. The main recording area was a large, low-ceilinged room with a drum kit in one corner screened off from the rest of the space.

The floor was dotted with mic stands bedecked with cables and wiring. The other room was the mixing room, which was the heart of the studio. On racks around the walls sat pieces of expensive-looking equipment with lots of knobs and flashing lights. There was the eight-track tape deck, a huge reel-to-reel machine in one corner and an ancient mixing desk taking up most of the room. This left just enough space for two chairs behind the desk and a sofa against the back wall. The rooms were separated by a glass partition.

The two guys who ran the studio, Kirt and Stevie, met us at the door to the mixing room and we all shook hands. Kirt was a symphony in denim – ripped jeans with his knees showing through, a denim shirt and denim jacket covered with badges. Stevie had green cropped hair and possessed what Jan thought was a very cool scar across his left cheek. This looked particularly weird because his face was otherwise unblemished, his features strikingly angelic. It was as though someone had flicked ash on a wet Botticelli.

We had of course been extremely ambitious in what we were aiming to do there. We had booked the studio for one eight-hour session to record four songs, citing the well-weathered fact that The Beatles had recorded their first album in twelve hours, so we should manage four songs in eight.

This was clearly not going to happen, and as we talked through the plan with Kirt, who seemed to be the organised one, we were soon persuaded to cut the project down to three songs. 'If The War Goes On', 'Already' and, of course, 'Angrenost' – the main reason for being there in the first place.

Recording is a complex business and we all secretly knew even in those days that we would be hard pressed to finish even one song in a day. After all, The Beatles may have recorded their first masterpiece in a day, but technology and production had moved on considerably since the early '60s. In fact we were playing pop stars in an era when excess was the watchword among the sort of bands we still admired. As we were setting up for our first session, The Clash and The Buzzcocks were recording great albums on the cheap down the road, but our role models were not the punk bands that had revolutionised pop music but the dinosaurs of the rock world who most sane critics were doing their best to put out of their misery. And those bands often took two years to record an album; our miserable one day they would have used to order the next consignment of coke or in setting up the tambourine sound for track one, side one.

We tried hard to get things going but what with the pressure of time and the knowledge that each hour there was costing us £20, we sort of froze. Luckily the two Tims were organised, and I only had to plug in an amp and guitar and Jan only had to open her mouth. The problem was Neil.

To record in a studio, the first thing you do is get the sounds of the instruments just right. Then you play through the basic song together – the drums, bass and guitar, say (and sometimes a rough vocal), but although these are recorded, only the drums are kept and the others are used merely as a guide. Then, you go back to the start, each musician records their instrument alone, and in this way the song is gradually built up. Finally the vocals and backing vocals are recorded.

In those days, long before digital recording was introduced, all these instruments and voices went on to a thick tape which contained separate bands for each instrument. So an eight-track recorder had eight bands. When all the parts were recorded this was played back through a mixing desk and the level of each sound adjusted through the song. Effects like reverb or echo or such delights as oral enhancers could be added and the whole soundscape was then recorded on to another tape, the final mix ready to be copied on to cassettes or on to vinyl in a cutting studio.

The perennial problem for any recording session was getting the drum sound as close to perfection as possible. Although many people think of drummers as the boneheads of any band (and this is usually a sound judgement) they are also almost without exception the prima donnas of the band. Forget the lead guitarist; yes, they are certainly egomaniacs when it comes to doing their solo or playing live when they want to outdo the vocalist, but they usually have complete mastery of their instrument and amplifier and know how to get their precious, unique sound right away. But drummers? According to most drummers, not only is their instrument subject to the most minute environmental changes during transport but the conditions of the room in which the drums are used also plays a major role in determining the sound they produce. The microphones have to be positioned just so, and the hi-hat or ride cymbals must not be in a draught. If too many Cubans jump up simultaneously from a game of dominoes, apparently this too can be terribly detrimental to the snare drum sound. I do believe chaos theory was created by a drummer.

And so the first three of our precious hours (or £60) in Crazy Sound Studios was taken up with Neil's peregrinations and the many refinements to his drum kit. By the time it was sorted out to his satisfaction, I was almost pulling my hair out and imagining the tape of our efforts as a mere drum track, which would have delighted Neil but done little to convince record executives.

But we did manage to get the three songs recorded in rough with the drum track down on each and we could then go back and do our bits individually. However, because time was pressing, we decided to do the individual instruments in pairs – if only one went well all the way through we would re-do the other; if both were perfect, we had saved time. Nice idea; the problem was that as the first pair to record bass and guitar, both Tim Alexander and I were hit by terminal nerves just as we were doing our first takes. Tim collapsed into a stuttering mess and I just couldn't make my hands work. It looked very much like the entire session was going to fall apart. Neil, who fancied himself as a guitarist on the quiet, made the subtle suggestion that he might do the guitar parts. Fortunately Jan could see I was about to go nuclear over this proposal and interceded by taking Neil aside and discussing the possibility that we might need a tambourine added to 'Angrenost' if we had a spare track after everything had been recorded.

Then Stevie had a great idea. A few seconds into Take 16 (or was it 17?) of the bass and guitar parts to 'Already', the first song Tim and I were attempting, the engineer jumped on the stop button and said, 'Okay, I think we all need a break. Michael, Tim, come with me.'

We followed him into the backyard of the building as the others milled around and Neil slunk away to an off-licence. The light was failing but it did nothing to disguise the mess in the yard. Pieces of old bike and some corrugated iron roofing were piled up at one end of the twelve-foot-square space, and crates of empty beer bottles and cartons sodden through and rotting kept the door to an outside toilet jammed shut.

Without saying a word, Stevie jumped up on to a low wall, took a tin from his pocket and began to roll a joint. I had never seen anyone do this before, and I couldn't believe how quickly he produced a carrot-sized roll-up. He lit it and it blazed for a second before he blew on the end and drew deeply on the spliff.

He assumed of course that we were used to smoking dope. The fact that neither Tim nor I had ever knowingly been in the same room as someone in the possession of any form of drug probably never entered Stevie's mind.

I remember a moment of anxiety as he handed the joint to me. What was I supposed to do with it? I couldn't bottle out – I was, after all (or so I imagined), momentarily at the epicentre of the pop world. No one had heard of me yet, but I was a guitarist in a band, in a recording studio, in London for God's sake; wasn't this exactly what I was supposed to be doing between takes? I took a long confident toke on the thing, tried to pretend to inhale and passed it on to Tim who I hoped (despite my affection for him) would fuck up completely and take the spotlight from me.

He didn't, and to this day I don't know whether he was being honest when he later told me it was his first time too. With a single relaxed self-confident motion, he drew in the smoke and inhaled, the bugger, before casually passing the joint back to Stevie.

I would like to say that the spliff made no difference to my performance, but in fact Stevie knew just what he was doing. He must have read the situation, known we were novices and rolled a really mild spliff that would simply relax us without spinning us out of control. Tim and I went back, recorded all three songs first take, and the day was saved.

By nine that night, eight hours and five minutes after arriving at Crazy Sound, we left with a couple of cassettes of the three finished songs and the master tape in a plastic bag. Despite having heard the songs at least fifty times during the session, we still played the tape for almost the entire two-hour journey home at ear-splitting volume, and, although I knew my sentiments were not shared by everyone in the van, I was convinced these were the best three songs anyone had ever recorded.

5

Of the three songs recorded at Crazy Sound only one was actually any good. 'Angrenost' was amateur and pretentious – a deadly combination. 'If The War Goes On' was a lame attempt at a rock song, but 'Already', a song for which Jan had written the lyrics about a woman getting ready for a special night out, was in an altogether different league and even today it still sounds like a song with potential. Sadly, that potential was never realised. But it almost happened.

From Neil we learned that the guys at Crazy Sound hadn't thought much of what we had done there, but the owner of the studio, a businessman named Boz Wilkins, who had heard the track, was impressed. One day about three weeks after returning from London we received a call from Boz who said he thought 'Already' was a great song and wondered if we had any plans for it. Naturally, we were interested in doing whatever we could with it and by happy chance we were throwing a party the following Saturday, a 1967 theme party, and so we invited along the whole team from Crazy Sound.

It turned out to be an educational evening. We held the party in our tiny basement flat and by ten the place was packed with about a fifty-fifty mix of people I knew and those I had never seen before in my life. The guys from the studio came along as promised, and even brought with them a starlet of their own, a young singer called Mel. Boz was, I guessed, about thirty, but looked older and bore a striking resemblance to Ray Davies of The Kinks. He wore a two-tone suit and an ultra-thin tie, he had his hair slicked back with lashings of gel and he chain-smoked. Mel was tall, blonde and undeniably gorgeous, if a little too knowing. She turned up in a silver mini-dress that barely covered red semi-transparent knickers (I checked a number of times just to make sure). She paired this with bright red basketball boots, and her hair was a huge mess described later by a not alto-gether unbiased Jan as 'a giant bird's nest', a style commonly known a few years later as 'Big Hair'.

Some of our old school friends home from university for the weekend also turned up. One of them applied the 1967 theme rather literally and came in junior school uniform, short trousers and cap, dressing as he had done during the Summer of Love. Neil arrived very late and brought with him a character I had seen on the periphery of the pop scene in Southend, a tall wiry guy wearing the tightest pair of jeans I had ever seen. Neil introduced him as Jed Fox. The name meant more than the face. Jed was semi-famous already and fronted a punk band who only the previous week had signed to A & M Records. I remember they had a song well known in Southend from their gigs called 'Shoot, Shoot' that had nothing to do with guns. I hated him of course.

Neil and Jed had brought three girls with them, all beau-tiful, leggy blondes, and within five minutes of arriving in the flat Jed was on our sofa with two of them, one kissing him hungrily on the mouth while the other was running a hand over the crotch of his absurd jeans.

But my most vivid memory of the evening was standing in the doorway to the kitchen looking out on to the familiar scene of our living room, now packed with bodies and strewn with beer cans. Stevie sat in one corner rolling a joint on a Barclay James Harvest album cover; in the opposite corner Neil was handing a huge spliff to one of his old friends from school. Mel was dancing with rather fabricated enthusiasm with Boz Wilkins, Jan was engrossed in conversation with the two Tims and young Jed was close to consummating his deeply emotional relationship with one of the two blondes. And at that moment, I suddenly felt very, very lonely.

In retrospect, I now realise 'lonely' is an inadequate adjective for the mixture of feelings I was experiencing at that moment. I thought I was lonely at the time but it wasn't that. As I looked out upon my peers, it suddenly struck me that up to that point in my life I had managed to get most things completely wrong. I was not yet twenty but I was living with someone, I was doing a degree course I neither enjoyed nor felt was leading anywhere, but most importantly, I was in a no-hope band, writing entirely the wrong sort of songs. I was completely and utterly out of step with my time. Whose idea was this party, for fuck's sake? My friend in the grey flannels and school tie had had the right idea – irony and disdain – whereas I was taking myself so bloody seriously. I knew then things had to change.

And in a most unexpected way, they did. Next morning, as we were clearing up and assessing the damage, Jan told me what Boz Wilkins had quietly mentioned to her the night before . . . Yes, he had liked our song, but he had no interest in me whatsoever.

I looked at her, confused. 'So, what does he want?' I asked, feeling slightly sick in the stomach.

'He wants his singer Mel and me to do it together, with him producing and using a band of session musicians.'

I must have turned a little pale, as Jan suddenly said, 'Are you okay?'

I nodded and sat down on the sofa, trying to avoid the various stains. 'What do you think?' I asked finally.

'I dunno,' she replied. 'I don't trust him, but then . . .'

'But what?'

'It could be a break for us, a start.'

'A break for *you* maybe,' I said with an anger I immediately regretted.

Jan smiled and touched my shoulder. 'Yeah, I know. I think maybe we should forget all about it.'

'No,' I replied, still with an unnecessary harshness to my voice. 'No, I insist, you call him. Call right now.' And although I didn't mean it, I must have sounded convincing.

'Are you sure?' Jan asked. And I could hear the thrill in her voice.

Somehow, I managed a weak smile. 'Just phone.'

Jan called the studio straight away. Stevie answered the phone and almost immediately I could hear Jan's voice began to betray disappointment, her initial enthusiasm seeping away to nothing.

Boz Wilkins had apparently left on a flight to New York that morning with Mel. They would be over there for at least four weeks, recording. And what of the song and Jan's collaboration? Apparently Stevie had shown no trace of compassion and spared no words of comfort telling her that on the way back to London Boz had changed his mind about the song and about Jan, because they had all left the party feeling she hadn't really been that interested in their proposal after all.

C

'She's always so smartly dressed, that's what I like about her,' said the young woman.

'Oh, I agree. And I think that's so important,' her friend replied.

It was the beginning of May 1979 and I was standing on the platform of Temple tube station, with its peeling paint and all-pervading stink of piss and lager, listening to two girls talking about Margaret Thatcher. Two days later she was Prime Minister.

It was the first election in which I could have participated, but I hadn't voted, had not the slightest interest in politics or politicians and found little common ground between my world-view and any of the official parties. It was a time in limbo. For me it seemed as though life in late 1970s Britain could become no more dislocated, no more miserable. Ever since childhood, the country had seemed on the verge of bankruptcy, lurching from one financial crisis to another – the three-day week, the power cuts, candles in the dark and a dead TV. And all this heaped upon a childhood, a time decades before political correctness, during which we were reminded constantly of our nation's glorious past. We had gone from pink on the map to red in the bank all in the space of a couple of generations. It felt as though the pendulum must shift, but no one then had the slightest inkling of what that would mean or where it would lead, except perhaps dear Margaret herself – but even that is doubtful.

Soon after, as things actually grew worse for a while, the naïve hope that the 1980s would be brighter, more satisfying and more successful became stronger, so that even I felt it. Amid the doom and listless hope, pop acquired a cynicism grown mature since the days of punk's primal scream. As the world was about to shift gear, we learned to reject not just the rules (that rebellion had been the preserve of the previous generation), but the inner structure, the ideologies from which rules are formed, the givens. We entered a new age of hedonism derived from a conviction that our lives would be short, our end violent, a conviction fuelled by pre-*glasnost* angst. And not too long after our Summer of Love party, I started wearing a badge that read 'FUCK ART, LET'S DANCE'.

1

It happens all the time, of course, and being dumped by Boz
Wilkins before we had even started was just the first of many
disappointments we had to accept as part of the learning
process. But this first time – like your first heartbreak,
maybe – affected us most intensely. Yet, at the same time, Mr
Boz Wilkins probably never knew quite how much of a
favour he had done me.

You see, no one is born cool. Most acquire cool and others
have it thrust upon them. After all, there must have been a
time when David Bowie jumped around his parents' living
room wearing pyjamas and playing air guitar, and Jarvis
Cocker has made a career from the fact that his mother sent
him to school in lederhosen.

Almost all pop stars learn how it's done by a process of
osmosis, almost subconsciously acquiring 'it', whatever 'it'
really is. And for me, late 1979 marked the time when I

finally tapped into the zeitgeist and my learning curve hit a
new, far steeper gradient.

It was obvious, even to me, that the world of pop music in
1979 had changed and was still in a tremendous state of flux,
and one thing that could be said for all the old progressive
rock bands I had admired was that they were most definitely
not in a state of flux.

I wasn't at all unusual in not liking punk. I could see why
people did like it, and in retrospect I understand the excitement and the energy and have gone back to buy albums I
hadn't then appreciated, but what immediately followed
punk was altogether different and much more interesting.
And when people of my generation proclaim that they were
punks, what most of them really mean is that around
1978–79 they got into New Wave.

New Wave really started happening in late 1978 and it
kept metamorphosing until it was overtaken by electro-pop
in the early '80s. And I first became aware of it when I finally
started listening to what Neil had to say instead of treating
him like a complete idiot. What I had mistaken for stupidity
was a deep and innate awareness of what pop music is really
about.

Neil was the first person I knew who bought *Never Mind
the Bollocks*, and he couldn't have been beaten by many
because he purchased it at 9 A.M. the morning of its release.
A few months earlier I remember asking him what the Sex
Pistols' first single sounded like (again he was the first person
I knew who had heard it), and his reply still impresses me as
just about the best description of 'Anarchy In The UK' I've
ever heard. He said: 'Imagine standing on the platform of
Leigh railway station and an inter-city goes by with someone
shouting out of the window at you. That's what it sounds
like . . . and it's fucking brilliant.'

Soon after our 1967 theme party the tumblers finally fell
into place and I very slowly began to acquire a sense of cool.

First to go were my Yes and Genesis albums. After my minor epiphany at the party I could hardly bear to even look at the cover of *Yessongs*. I had almost no money so I couldn't replace my record collection overnight even if I had known exactly what to buy. Instead, I bought a dozen C-90s and gave them to Neil with instructions to tape the twenty-four albums he most liked.

And so I began to catch up, and soon I had the cream of the crop: The Jam's first album, *All Mod Cons*, Siouxsie and the Banshees, The Cure's *Seventeen Seconds*, Television's *Marquee Moon* and the first two Talking Heads LPs, Patti Smith, The Clash's *London Calling* and a collection of John Peel sessions featuring what were then obscure recordings by Joy Division, Echo and the Bunnymen and The Fall.

This was a whole new world. Everyone and their granny knew of and had probably heard a snatch or two of the Pistols, but this was the new alternative scene, the re-ignited ashes from punk's self-combustion. In the following years there would appear Ph.D. theses and rock histories by writers such as Greil Marcus and Jon Savage exploring the phenomenon of Punk and New Wave and how one segued into the other, but nothing can capture the raw excitement, the emotional liberation of waking up one morning to Yes and by the afternoon stubbing out a joint on their vinyl while listening at top volume to The Jam screaming out 'Down In The Tube Station At Midnight'.

This revelation and the internal revolution I experienced was so powerful I was numbed by it. I couldn't pick up a guitar for weeks (by now the railway sleeper had returned to junk-shop-land and been replaced by a hard-saved-for Strat copy). I certainly couldn't write a note or contemplate forming a new band or recording new songs. Which is I suppose an odd reaction considering the times now-famous pop stars tell us they were inspired by a Clash gig or a Jam album and formed their first band the very next day.

The numbness eventually ebbed away and with it went all notions of forming the sort of band I had once struggled to hold together. With it went all thoughts of acoustic guitars, poetic lyrics and twenty-minute opuses. On the very fringe of what was then happening (by now we had gone through Christmas and New Year and had entered the new decade) was a sound I told myself I had been searching for my entire life. It was a sound coming from some of the rarer Peel sessions. It hadn't even made vinyl at the time, but was lurking there under the surface, ready to break, and it spoke to me directly.

I knew I would never feel comfortable thrashing a guitar in a garage band imitating The Jam or The Clash, but some of these new bands were experimenting with synthesisers and drum machines and they were completely alien to musicians such as Keith Emerson of ELP, who used the synth to compose grandiose pseudo-classics. These bands were using electronics in an altogether more vital, exciting way, linking up with dance rhythms and using simple but powerful motifs. It was the sound of the new decade, the sound of the future and the future was where I wanted to be. 'FUCK ART, LET'S DANCE'.

!

Jan and I bought our first drum machine and synthesiser in February 1980, a few days before my twenty-first birthday, and it was without doubt the best decision we ever made.

Of course we had very little money and were both living on university grants, which then together totalled a staggering £2,000 per year, but we had friends who to us were enormously rich and who, we hoped, would act as guarantors for a loan. We approached Neil first – after all, he had a job and a flashy car – but he refused on the grounds that he would never in a thousand years help us buy, as he put it, 'a fucking bastard drum machine'. We realised secretly (and he knew all along) that he would never have convinced a credit company anyway because he had only been working for a year. Nothing more was said, but we then turned to a family friend who had also been my junior school teacher. I had renewed contact with him and his girlfriend a year earlier and we had become good friends.

Colin was in his early forties at the time, but he was so hip that both Jan and I, over twenty years his junior, could only aspire to be as cool as him. He lived in a small terraced cottage in the heart of Old Leigh, overlooking the harbour. The house was all pine and distressed furniture, chocolate-coloured walls and polished floorboards. Colin had every Beatles, Stones and Dylan album released and some on special import. He and his common-law wife, Christine, brewed strong black Lavazza when all we had ever tasted was Nescafé and they left copies of *Penthouse* and Italian *Vogue* lying casually on the coffee-table in the living room.

Once we convinced him it really was what we wanted to do and that we could afford about £20 per month for three years to pay for the stuff, Colin was more than happy to support our loan and within days the equipment was taking pride of place in the sitting room of our flat in Grand Parade.

It is staggering to think what we got for our money. We were paying off £600 for a drum machine and string synthesiser, plus about £150 interest on the loan. The drum machine was supposed to be the Rolls-Royce of drum machines at the time, but now it is literally a museum piece, a Roland, the first commercially available beatbox. It sounded like the rabbit in the Duracell ads, but tinnier. It was pre-digital, non-programmable and had about forty different rhythms ranging from the insipid to the turgid; but it was a drum machine, which meant we no longer needed to rely on drummers like Neil. We were beginning to approach what we thought was a 'modern' pop sound, what bands in the *NME* referred to as 'post-industrial'.

The string synth really was a lovely machine. Very simple to use, it had a collection of beautiful string sounds and when it was put through a reverb unit, it was simply sex on a stick. But even so, its price tag still amazes me. Today you could buy a digital synth with over a thousand voices, internal sequencers, maybe even sampling power, a drum machine built in that sounds indistinguishable from a real drummer and is fully programmable, the whole lot built around an eight-track recorder, all for less than we paid two decades ago for a crap beatbox and a simplistic keyboard.

However, none of this mattered in February 1980 – those were the market prices and the best money could buy this side of professional equipment owned by the likes of Phil Collins or Fleetwood Mac. What was crucial was that it enabled us to write the sort of songs we wanted to start writing and to create a semblance of the sound we were chasing.

This was monumental enough, but other things changed dramatically the week the new equipment arrived. Without telling Jan, I went to a barber's shop and had my hair cut. And boy, what a cut. Since entering the sixth form at a liberal school I had allowed my hair to grow. By February 1980 it was past my shoulders, straggly and often greasy. So, to accompany the new sound, I had a crewcut, almost a scalping, known in the trade as a Number One.

I loved it and could hardly stop rubbing my head as I strolled back whistling from the barber one unseasonably warm February afternoon. I walked into the flat and when Jan saw me she was rooted to the spot.

To say she was not impressed would be the severest understatement. She would not talk to me for the rest of the day or that night, and only gradually did she accept the fact that the deed was done. But something about my new look must have worked, for the following Saturday she completely turned the tables on me. Telling me she was popping out to see a friend, she returned two hours later, her waist-length hair in a clear plastic bag which she deposited with great aplomb on the coffee-table next to the new synth, and asked me what I thought of her bob.

And so began a completely new phase in our career. Armed with new equipment, new ideas and perhaps most importantly, new hair-dos, we were off the starting block. To me, this was actually the beginning of my musical career.

What was so great about the new gear was not just the sounds we could make but the fact that it attracted all the right attention from other musicians we knew. Most important of these was Martin Jago, who had been a friend of ours for a long time, but who only became interested in us as musicians when we changed into this new musical creature.

Martin was at Sussex University and was a really solid bass player. He also looked fantastic. He was about six-two and weighed maybe three pounds. He had receding hair cut really short in a Howard Devoto (of Magazine) style, wore baggy black clothes and round glasses and had a deep resonant voice completely at odds with his appearance.

We were still on the best of terms with Tim Alexander, who had been our part-time bass player, but his own band, Fragment, were entering a new, active phase and he didn't really go for what we were trying to do and so Martin stepped into his shoes.

This line-up became the core of the new musical entity that February. I concentrated on playing synth and chipping in the odd bit of guitar (which was still and to this day remains the only instrument I can play properly, but was then a less fashionable instrument than a synth). Jan had put her flute into a box at the bottom of the wardrobe; she sang and played synthesiser (when I wasn't); Martin played bass.

The only thing we hadn't organised was a new name.

Bands spend an inordinately long time thinking up a name. I've even known groups who did nothing in their entire careers other than think about their name – they wrote nothing and played nothing but went through at least fifteen hundred different names, never settling upon one before 'splitting up'. With hindsight it is clear this over-emphasis on names is time and effort wasted. A name is a name is a name, and once fame strikes, whether or not a name is good or bad or even appropriate, is irrelevant. If this was not the case, how did 10,000 Maniacs, The Buzzcocks or The Police ever succeed?

But, like every other band we had ever known or came to know, we deliberated long into the night for weeks on end before the three of us hit upon the name Watch With Mother.

The name had some significance to us. First of all it had been the name of a tea-time kids' slot on TV when we were young children and would mean something to everybody our age, but most importantly it resonated well with a theme we were beginning to build into our new image. Jan had become interested in indoctrination. She was doing some psychology and education units in her course at Goldsmith's College and had started writing lyrics about how as children we were all indoctrinated to believe certain things, and Watch With Mother fitted neatly with this.

Then, a friend of ours who was in the middle of an art foundation course at the local poly came up with the idea of designing a logo for us, which consisted of a baby's face with a microchip and wires positioned just above the eyebrows. The night she came round to the flat with the first drawing of this image I felt a tingle of excitement run down my spine and could sense things at last coming together. In the subsequent months this image appeared all over Southend and beyond as it was reproduced on specially prepared letterheads, posters and even cheaply made badges we sold at gigs.

As the new look was falling into place and the three of us began to sense we were on the right commercial path, we had the little matter of songwriting to take care of. Luckily, the excitement generated by all this frantic activity was immensely inspiring in other ways. Almost all my time was now taken up at the drum machine and synth, and occasionally the guitar. The sitting room in the flat was permanently scattered with notepads, scraps of lyrics and sheets of music

interspersed with coiled leads, effects boxes we had begged
and borrowed and mains extension leads. After rehearsals
the place stank of beer and the musky odour of cannabis.
God only knows what the landlady, who lived on the floor
above, must have thought. But such things seemed irrelevant as we forged a musical revolution.

The songs we composed during that period were suitably
up-tempo but also appropriately pared to the musical bone.
We were taking as our cue some of the new German bands,
the grandchildren of hippies like Tangerine Dream and pop
like Kraftwerk, groups such as Noi and DAF. This we
blended with the early Echo and the Bunnymen and Gang of
Four singles and, of course, the first Joy Division album,
Unknown Pleasures.

After a few months of intense writing we were feeling
pretty pleased with ourselves, but then, in the summer of
1980, Joy Division released 'Love Will Tear Us Apart' and
we were struck by just how flimsy our efforts had been. One
night, hit by a sudden paroxysm of inadequacy, the three of
us ceremoniously destroyed all trace of what we had done
and returned to the drawing-board.

A dramatic gesture, yes (although it was inspired by too
many joints on my part, and for the whole of the next morning we regretted what we had done), but within days Watch
With Mother were writing far better material and a few
months later we had a set of new songs that we believed
stood comparison with what we were hearing on John Peel
and on the new albums and singles we were buying. What's
more, the great beauty of this set-up – three people using
exclusively electronic equipment – was that we could make
what we thought at the time were reasonable recordings in
our living-room.

We borrowed a two-track reel-to-reel tape recorder, the
sort my father owned during the early '70s, upon which he
played endless tapes of Acker Bilk and Shirley Bassey. It was

a crude device, but of infinitely better quality than a cassette player. We had a tiny mixer a friend made for us for £5. It was about the size of a shoe box, with four holes on one side and two on the other. Four sliders on the top allowed you to alter the level of each input, but nothing else. Into this we fed the drum machine, the synth, Martin's bass and sometimes my guitar. These went on to one of the two tracks of the tape recorder, and Jan's voice we put through a cheap mic from a portable cassette player on to the other track. It was the most primitive recording studio in the world, except perhaps for the ingenious 'mics on chair-backs' of our 'dancing in chain-mail' days. But because of the sort of music we were trying to produce, it actually ended up sounding not at all bad.

We had latched on to phrases bandied around by the music press of the time, in particular the expressions 'bleak and industrial' and 'pale and meaningful', and applied them religiously to everything we did; the way we looked, the way we presented ourselves and the music we composed. Rough edges in the mix were therefore fine, cool even; besides, the sheer beauty of any chord played on the string synth once it was passed through a reverb unit over-rode any of the cruder sounds. But best of all, with the drum machine there was no longer any need to spend four hours getting a bass drum sound from a real drummer. And the drum machine didn't drink and wouldn't have tried to grope my girlfriend if it did.

One weekend during autumn 1980 we decided we were ready to make the definitive recording of what we had been working on, and so a tape named simply Watch With Mother with the baby's face on the cover was produced. It contained four songs: 'Atom Bombs And Human Beings', 'Sleeping', 'The Line' and a cover of a song we had all placed at the top of our list of favourites, 'Psycho Killer' by Talking Heads.

We listened to the finished product perhaps a million times the following week, not giving a thought to what we were supposed to do with it now it was done. We all loved it, and we played it to our friends, some of whom shared our enthusiasm, some who decidedly did not. And it was only after at least seven days of saturation playing of those four songs that the thought struck us that perhaps we had only just completed the first and maybe easiest stage of the process. Now we had to play the tape to the people who mattered. It was time to approach the record industry.

9

How do I put this without sounding embittered? A & R men (those responsible for what is quaintly termed 'Artists & Repertoire') have to listen to a lot of music from thousands of hopefuls, so they are overwhelmed by it all. No? Okay: A & R men are only human, they make mistakes. Nope, that doesn't wash. Right: A & R men have their own taste and it might not coincide with what you produce. Or what about: A & R men have to obey their bosses? No.

All right, okay, this is all dishonest crap. Let me tell you the truth: A & R men are stupid. No, even this is too measured – let's lay it on the line and present the brutal facts: A & R men are the most stupid, blinkered, unimaginative bunch of failed-musicians-who-believe-they-are-God-all-fucking-mighty-scum-bag-filth you should think yourself lucky you will probably never, ever meet. The only consolation for the humiliation they dished out was that within a few years of their rejection I was earning more in one month than they were in twelve. There, now that's out of my system (twenty years on), I realise I *am* embittered, horribly so.

Even as recently as 1980, A & R men were willing to have young unknowns turn up in their offices to play their tapes. This was a tradition begun in the '60s when bands actually performed live for record executives after setting up their amps and drums in the company offices. Today it is entirely different; no one gets in through the door unless they are already famous, have a manager with clout, or offer said A & R man large sums of cash, drugs or both.

With the hopes of the innocent, I went along to see what these people would think of Watch With Mother, the tape, the band, the concept, the whole shebang. We had made ten copies of the tape, Jan had sent three to ads in the *NME* – 'New Label Seeks Brilliant Artists', and we sent off four to London venues to try to get a few gigs.

The way to approach a record label was to write to them telling them about the band, enclosing a photo and asking for a meeting. Martin wrote four letters to major labels, including one to a friend who worked at A & M Records, and I contacted another three, Chrysalis, EMI and Rough Trade. The understanding was that if there were any responses, whoever had made contact would handle the meeting. Of mine, only EMI responded, but when we received their letter asking me to come to their office a week later, our excitement was almost uncontainable.

And so I found myself one cold morning walking into the Central London offices of EMI and asking for the A & R department. I should have been in an Inorganic Chemistry lecture, but did Chuck Berry ever worry about such things?

It was to be my first deflating experience with a major label.

John Seagrove's office was, I later realised, a perfect cliché

for the time – all bachelor steel and leather, the most expensive-looking hi-fi I had ever seen, a few white lilies in a glass
vase personally arranged by Mapplethorpe perhaps, and a
very, very big, fuck-you desk. Behind it sat the diminutive
figure of Mr Seagrove.

Of course I was intimidated. Johnboy was my age, and
although when I look back upon the meeting I realise that he
had a face that would make William Hague look rugged,
there was no getting away from the fact that he was my age.
I just couldn't stop thinking, 'Look at him and look at me.' I
had the option of hiding behind the ageless image of the
artist, the poor student, the working-class kid with God-
given talent, but it was very difficult in that office.

He didn't get up, never feigned friendship and only
exuded minimal interest in me being there at all. 'Good of
you to come,' he said with about as much sincerity as Billy
Graham. 'Take a seat and let's have a listen to your
product.'

Cringing at the word 'product', I handed over the cassette
and started making all manner of excuses for the sound quality, the cover, the quality of the tape copier, the hiss, US
involvement in Nicaragua, the lot. He ignored it all, swung
round casually to the tape machine following a routine he
had performed bored so many times, and I felt like crawling
away and hiding between his secretary's legs.

The tape began to turn, the hiss kicked in and he turned
to adjust a control. Then the first song, 'Sleeping', started
up, the drum machine's patter and the string synth. His face
was totally expressionless. He reached for the volume control and zapped it up so that the walls were almost shaking.
And it was then that I really appreciated what a fantastic job
this guy had. He listened to music all day at ear-splitting
volume, and even if he hated most of it it was better than
working in a factory or an office. He got paid well, met loads
of women, needed no qualifications or talent, and yes, I

keep coming back to it, he listened to music very loudly for a living.

And then the music stopped. I was brought out of my reverie with shocking suddenness . . . What was he doing? The song was only a minute through. I looked up with what must have been a horrified expression on my face, but dear John didn't flinch. He span the tape on to the next song, 'Atom Bombs And Human Beings' and pressed 'play'.

The music burst through the speakers, the eerie opening sounds of backwards screaming then the bass and drums and the guitar chopping away. Jan started to sing. The A & R man listened to a few bars and then, picking up the tape case with one hand and turning the stereo down with the other, I heard him mutter: '"Psycho Killer"?' Because of the volume of the music, I couldn't make out the tone of his voice, but for the first time he showed some facial expression . . . and I'm sure it was mirth.

The tape stopped again and we sat without speaking as it squeaked fast-forward and stopped a few bars into the Talking Heads cover. He sat back, flicking up the volume again, touched his fingertips together, arched them under his chin and looked at the ceiling. I looked at the edge of the desk. There was silence again.

I looked up just in time to see him flip the tape into the case and spin it through the air towards me.

'You don't like it,' I ventured.

'No,' he said, and there was that same absence of expression in his voice. 'Very dated, I'm afraid.'

I was stunned. 'Dated!'

'Yeah, you heard any new stuff recently? And I don't mean this Joy Division, Bunnymen shit. They're so, so . . . yesterday. Get into the New Romantics, Mike. That's the future.'

I refused to show my ignorance, but he was on a roll anyway.

'I had a band in here last week. I almost got them too, but

they slipped through my fingers. Called Vertigo Dawn. Going to be fucking huge, Mike . . . Chrysalis just paid half a mill for 'em.'

I didn't know what to say. I had never heard of Vertigo Dawn or the New Romantics. And anyway, I hated being called Mike by people who didn't know me, especially short people with bum-fluff. But before I could say anything John Seagrove was out of his chair and walking round to my side of the desk. It was obvious the interview was over.

'Get into the New Romantics,' he repeated. 'And then maybe we can meet up again. That girl, what's her name? Jill?'

'Jan.'

'Yeah, Jane, she's got potential.'

And I was in reception again with the door closed behind me and the tape in my hand.

10

It was a massive disappointment, but to be expected really. The number of bands who have been given big deals after walking into record company offices with tapes is, well . . . zero, I think. But we had to try, just as all young bands try. There is nothing to lose but your dignity. But then the loss of dignity was, as always, painful to take.

Actually, not all A & R men were quite so unhelpful. I once got to see an executive at an independent who had a tiny office on Carnaby Street. The boss met me at the door and showed me to his little office, we had a chat and I played him my tape. He made no comment about it but put on what he said was a test copy of a record he was planning for release a few weeks later, a slice of vinyl fresh from the pressing plant. He handed me the demo cover and I read: 'Young Guns (Go For It!)' by a group called Wham! Then, just as the music started up, a young, good-looking guy with thick dark hair poked his head around the door to the office and asked us both if we would like tea. The record executive called him over and introduced me to the new arrival. 'Mike,' he said proudly, looking at me and hugging the guy. 'This is one of our Young Guns.' Both of us a little embarrassed, we shook hands, then George Michael smiled and wandered off to make me tea.

The fact is, there was a great disparity between what we thought was good commercial music and what others with clout thought was good commercial music. But it is also fortunate we didn't realise this, for there were other opportunities to be forged.

Our efforts were ignored by almost everyone, and twenty years on, I've still only heard from one of the record companies (apart from EMI) we wrote to that undignified February. But, that one exception was the reply that did change things.

To our astonishment and delight, we received a response from *NME*'s 'New Label Seeks Brilliant Artists', who thought we were, well . . . brilliant.

Jan took the call from a guy calling himself Yvette Döll (we later learned his name was actually Greg Carlin), who thought we had the perfect sound for a compilation album he was putting together. His label was called Deutche Phonograph, which was of course a take on a famous German label (a play on words a little like that used by the manufacturers of my all-time favourite musical product, the £30 Fender Stratocaster copy called a Fander Stratocoaster).

Greg was keen to see us play live and sounded terribly serious and enthusiastic about what we were doing. Fortunately, our disappointment over my seminal A & R experience had been tempered only that morning when Jan had succeeded in persuading the manager of the Rock Garden in Covent Garden to let us play there.

So, not only did we have this Mr Döll insisting that we were set for superstardom, we could actually tell him we were playing in London a few weeks later. Jan put down the phone and looked positively lit up with excitement. I remember the three of us, Martin, Jan and I, dancing around the room.

11

When you're trying to get somewhere in music, there are certain milestones to reach for. Your first guitar, drum kit or bass; your first tape; your first concert. Then there are iconic targets, the next level to be attained by the avatar: your first interview at a record company, your first time in a recording studio and your first gig in London.

During the early 1980s there were new venues appearing and disappearing every week in London and the *NME* and *Melody Maker* were filled with hundreds of adverts for bands, famous, infamous and unknown, all publicising their gigs. But most of these venues were insignificant – in fact, if you ignored the big places, like Wembley Stadium, there were only a handful of venues everyone knew were frequented regularly by record company executives and scouts. Of these the attainable ones for a band without management or a deal already were Dingwalls, the 100 Club, and most famous of them all, the Rock Garden.

And when you're young and ambitious and dying to play at the Rock Garden, you have the most amazing fantasies about the place. Sadly, when you reach such career landmarks they are almost always horribly disappointing. The manager of the Rock Garden, like that of most small London venues, didn't really want bands to play at his venue, he would rather have just had an all-night disco; such things attracted more people, the overheads were lower and he ran a substantially reduced risk of some drummer or bassist vomiting down his frilly shirt. But the Rock Garden and the other venues kept on bands in order to maintain a tradition dating back to early BB King gigs and the first Rolling Stones concerts; they saw themselves (quite rightly) as an integral part of British rock history.

Consequently, every aspiring musician had to play the Rock Garden, but the rewards, at least the immediate ones, were slender indeed.

The deal was this: we sold tickets for the gig at £3.50 a time, from which we would keep 10 whole pennies per ticket. We had to supply the sound engineer, tip the DJ who opened and closed the evening, arrange our own transport from Southend to London and do our own local advertising. The Rock Garden placed an ad in the *NME* and we had a slot first on the bill of four bands and the chance of being spotted by Mickie Most.

And the venue itself? In better days it had been a wine cellar. It was accessed by a winding staircase down which before the show we had to carry our amps, keyboards and assorted machines and up which, three-quarters stoned, we had to carry them after the show. The changing room was actually a toilet shared by all four bands and the stage was the size of a child's trampoline. But it was the Rock Garden and it was a fantastic honour to play there.

That first London show will remain with me for the rest of my life. Okay, we made £9 from the ninety friends and family we persuaded to come in two coaches from Southend and had to pay £33 for the van hire and the sundry costs of putting on the show, but it was one of the most exciting, sweaty, noisy, energised evenings any of us could have wished for.

Ninety fans was pretty good for a first show in London and the Rock Garden is not large. With the early arrivals for the other groups, the place was two-thirds full by the time we came on at 7.30, and as the set progressed more people arrived and very few left, which encouraged us no end.

And that night we were really on form. By then we had played a couple of gigs in pubs in Southend with mixed results, we had gained some experience and that had shown us what was going to go down well and what wasn't. The three-piece arrangement worked perfectly and convinced us that we did not need a drummer. Jan was in control of the drum machine, played most of the synth parts and sang lead vocal, while I switched from guitar to keyboard for different songs and tried my best with minimal backing vocals and Martin chugged away on bass. Considering the slender line-up, we made a pretty punchy noise, and after the first song, the place was heaving.

Our set was short but up-tempo and energetic, and when we came to the end of the last song, 'Sleeping', we actually got an encore. I couldn't believe it. Suddenly we were back on stage and I was thrashing out the opening chords to 'Psycho Killer', and the place just erupted. I had never felt such a burst of energy before. To look down at the audience and see a heaving mass of sweaty bodies, a single organism pulsing in time to the music, was an experience worth every moment of effort, set-backs and depression.

Of course I was not to know then where all this was leading. At that moment I could feel nothing but a fantastic rush, a high no drug could emulate, and my only thought was that I loved this and wanted to do this over and over again, that I would never be satisfied by doing anything else again. And when we finished, with the crazy noise of distorted guitar at the end of the song, and the notes fading away, what was now an audience 150-strong made a noise I had never before heard.

We met Yvette (or Greg) in the pub along the street after the show. We were so hyped up I don't know how we came across, but we knew then that it didn't matter. My memory of the evening was all the show, the sound of that crowd, the buzz, and I can hardly recall a word from the conversation in the pub.

Of course Greg was impressed and even more excited by what we were doing. He had reservations about certain aspects of our set and liked some songs more than others, but he was really keen.

It turned out that Yvette was another rock 'n' roll cliché, an ex-junky who had lived in Berlin during the '70s, claimed he had produced some tapes for Lou Reed and Iggy Pop, and even tried to have us believe he had once been a friend of Warhol's. I never discovered what was true about Greg and what was false. His pseudonym kept changing and it just happened to have been Yvette Döll the week he called us. It could just as easily have been Dag Dag, Chakk or Voice of Sudeten Creche. Greg used his persona a bit like we used the band. We expressed parts of ourselves in our group names and our music, while he played the chameleon game with himself.

Whoever the true Greg Carlin may have been, none of us really cared that night. We drove back in the hired van and off-loaded the gear at the flat, lay on the floor with cups of tea and a joint and waited for *Tiswas* to start on TV, and all we could think of was the reception we had received and the fact that Greg wanted us to record two songs for a compilation album to be distributed throughout Europe and the US. Suddenly it seemed like things were starting to work out.

12

Things continued to go well for some time after the Rock Garden gig and within a few weeks we found ourselves with a series of dates in London.

One Saturday we were booked at a club in Soho. We spent some of the afternoon in London, just hanging out, posing. Parking the van in a side-street, Jan, Martin and I walked the length of King's Road just to feel part of the scene. We had dressed up specially. Jan wore skin-tight purple leopard-skin trousers and tucker boots, Martin was in black jeans and sprayed-on black string vest, and I wore eye make-up and had on a T-shirt carrying a fluorescent picture of Margaret Thatcher sticking two fingers up. We thought we were ultra-cool, but after ten minutes of the King's Road we suddenly felt incredibly self-conscious, not because of any outrage we had caused, but the opposite – everyone else posing in Chelsea was so extreme we had begun to feel like bank clerks.

The gig that night turned out to be in the basement of a brothel. The place stank so much I could not tell one smell from another – and I was doing a chemistry degree. As we unloaded the gear, we watched the hookers plying their trade and I didn't know whether to feel good or bad. We were doing what all bands had done for decades, serving our apprenticeship in dives like this, following in the honourable tradition of every band you've ever heard of; but part of me wondered whether we were actually any different from Cucumber Lill standing on the corner.

The venue was tiny and because it was a basement the ceiling was ridiculously low and pillars obscured half the stage. About thirty minutes before going on, the place was deserted and we stood at the bar with the lead singer from the main band, trying to cheer each other up. The singer was a friendly guy who seemed determined not to let anything get him down. He talked incessantly and did cheer us up. But he was obsessed with insects. He wouldn't stop talking about them, how the world depended upon insects, fascinating details about their habits, their likes and dislikes. I couldn't decide whether he was joking, a genius or mad.

Later, a few people wandered into the club, although I'm sure some had taken a wrong turn at the entrance upstairs, and by the time we went on there was an audience of perhaps twenty. After we left the stage to a smattering of applause, the main band went on and our singer friend turned out to be an amazing performer. But every song was about insects, especially ants.

One Thursday not so long after that night, we turned on the TV and there was the band we had supported in Soho and the insect-obsessed singer, Adam Ant. And so we learned a new lesson – it is sometimes only a small step from playing under a brothel to appearing on *Top of the Pops*.

A few months later I arrived back from a rare trip to college to learn from Jan that we had been offered a support slot at an end-of-term gig at Southend Polytechnic. The gig had come from the Rock Garden show because the Ents Officer of the poly had caught the end of our set. He wanted us to support some group from Basildon none of us had ever heard of called Depeche Mode.

We knew we'd be on a big stage and that there would be a large audience, but because we had never heard of Depeche Mode (and not many people had in April 1981) we didn't get unduly excited about playing support at Southend Poly.

The concert itself was no great event. We went on very early and the main hall was only about a quarter full. We were received enthusiastically by our group of fans, but the main body of people there seemed quite uninterested in what we were doing. I was relieved to get off the stage and hit the bar. But then halfway through my first pint, I heard the DJ announce the main band and I wandered back.

The place was now over half-full and I could feel an indefinable air of excitement. I realised then that this Depeche Mode obviously had a sizeable and loyal following. There was a certain arrogance about their fans. They looked quite different from the Watch With Mother devotees, and indeed the members of Watch With Mother themselves. These boys and girls were wearing *a lot* of make-up. Martin and I quite often wore eye-liner, but this was something else: they had bright swatches of colour across their cheeks and heavily painted eyelids, like something from a Venetian carnival. We were wearing dark greys and black, tight trousers, Doc Marten's and old macs; they were flouncing around in rich purples and orange to complement their make-up, the boys in frilly shirts and baggy trousers tucked into ankle boots, the girls bedecked with heavy jewellery and wearing tight satin skirts, billowing blouses and ornate waistcoats.

This was the time when Thatcher and Reagan were at

their cuddliest, when Brixton was a-riot, there was shit-smearing in the Maze prison and Peter Sutcliffe confessed. It was also the start of the New Romantic era and for an old post-industrialist like me it came as a bit of a culture shock.

And then the bass drum beat started up and the band appeared on stage in what looked like *Thunderbirds* outfits. But it wasn't the sartorial inclinations of Depeche Mode that surprised me . . . I just couldn't believe the bass drum sound. I looked for the drummer, but there was no sign of a kit on the stage. Then the snare came in and I was completely thrown, this was just the best drum sound I had ever heard. And no drummer. Finally all the synths came tumbling into the song and the lead singer, Dave Gahan, launched into 'New Life'.

I can't say I ever liked Depeche Mode's music much – it was too flimsy and sugar-coated for me. But there's no denying it worked. In fact I heard the other day that they have so far sold 35 million albums, so who cares what I think? But as much as I did not like them and felt irritated by their ridiculous catchiness, I was utterly blown away by their professionalism and the quality of their sound. It was so clear halfway through the first verse of 'New Life' that this band were going to be huge. And this, we learned backstage an hour later, was one of their first gigs.

We also discovered they had not yet been tarnished by adulation. Andy Fletcher was painfully reserved, in fact he said almost nothing, while Dave Gahan was very wrapped up in being an embryonic pop star and even in those days was the most keen to get absolutely stoned out of his mind at the earliest opportunity. He was later to 'die' three times after heroin overdoses in LA, but came bouncing back as a serious pop force during the late '90s. Martin Gore was more cerebral, quiet but not closed in upon himself; he was happy to chat to you if you had something worth saying. But of all of them, Vince Clarke was the only one I could later call a friend.

Vince was the brains behind the earliest incarnation of Depeche Mode and acted as principal songwriter and producer, although to give him credit, Martin went on to be a very good songwriter too and took the band to superstardom, steering their sound away from the bubblegum pop of those early days.

Getting to know Depeche Mode was, by pure accident, perfect timing for us because they were then on a very steep ascendant and we were not too proud to try to jump on their coat-tails. They had just signed a record deal with Mute Records and 'New Life' was about to hit the shops (it would soon go to Number 22 in the charts and launch their careers). They also had a succession of gigs lined up for which they needed a support band. And they liked us.

A week after the gig at the poly in Southend, I picked up the phone at our flat and heard Dave Gahan the other end of the line wondering if we would like to support them at The Venue in London. Could I drop in a tape of our stuff to pass on to the gig organisers? I was staggered. The Venue (sadly no longer in existence) was a 1,000-seater theatre near Victoria Station and one of the most prestigious places to play in London, This, I was convinced, would be our Big Break.

The next morning I set off for Basildon, where all the members of Depeche Mode lived with their parents. I suppose I must have been early, or maybe Dave and the boys had been playing in London the night before, but it seemed to take for ever to rouse anyone at the address I had been given. Finally, as I turned to head back to the railway station feeling confused and depressed, the door to the house opened and the lead singer of Depeche Mode stood there in a short, ragged dressing-gown he was holding together at the waist. He looked as though he had been dragged from a hospital ward and propped up at the door. Rubbing his eyes, he stared at me, recognition finally dawning as I handed him the tape.

'Oh, cheers, man,' he said, his voice rasping as it never had, or would, on record. I caught a glimpse of his mother crossing the narrow hall behind him and for a microsecond I thought there might be the chance of a cup of tea and a chat about the trials and tribulations of trying to get somewhere in the world of pop. But no. Dave smiled, said he'd get back to me a.s.a.p., waved a feeble 'bye' and slowly closed the door.

Two weeks later we were on stage supporting Depeche Mode at The Venue, but it did not turn out to be the great dream we had imagined it would be. The audience were almost totally unaware of our existence. We plodded through our set, each song receiving diminishing responses until only a smattering of claps came from our vastly out-numbered cadre of fans who had again loyally travelled up from Southend.

Backstage, Depeche Mode felt genuinely sorry for us, saying nice things about our set and that the fans were perhaps only there to see them, which sounds conceited but was actually right on the money. Again, we went out front to see the band perform and again we were knocked out by their sound, which was, if anything, even better than the first time we had heard them. And between the poly gig and this one, 'New Life' had charted.

The audience went wild in their rather fey, New Romantic way. There was no screaming or ripping up of seats but raucous applause and rather fabricated hysteria every time Dave opened his mouth or Vince played a particularly catchy little melody.

The funny thing about Depeche Mode, and something that was borne out by their later global success, was that they were far better than their audience deserved. The New Romantic crowd were the worst sort of pop fans – they were far more interested in themselves and what their friends thought about their lip-gloss than in the bands they followed.

Of course they applauded and cheered and, most crucially, they bought records and tickets, but it was all really a pose and Depeche Mode were as disposable as a tube of bright red lipstick.

Depeche Mode knew this. By the time of the Venue gig in July 1981 they were obviously on the brink of massive success if only they could keep their heads. But there were also huge pressures beginning to bear down on them. They were getting into some serious drugs; backstage at The Venue was how I imagined the back room at The Factory must have looked fifteen years earlier, or the inside of a Rolling Stones hotel room in the mid-1970s. Dave was hollow-eyed and wired before they played and some of the others in their entourage appeared to be in varying stages of pharmaceutically-induced otherworldliness. Yet, when they performed they played perfectly, and went through their polished and practised set as though they had been abusing themselves for years.

There were clearly other strains between the members of the band. They all knew their sound had a very limited life expectancy and that they would have to develop and grow. However, Andy seemed worried because he couldn't write a note and was dependent upon the other three, once confiding to me that he was envious of Martin, Jan and me because we would soon have university degrees to fall back on whereas he only had a couple of O-levels to his name. 'If this band fails,' he told me, 'I'm finished.' But it didn't.

Dave Gahan probably would have thought the same as Andy if he had stopped to think about it at all, but he was so confident I don't think he ever did. Dave was never the world's most extrovert frontman, but it takes a certain strength of character to get up on stage and sing, and that steeliness gave him all the belief in himself he needed. He was also the one who received most of the adulation and that, as I had already learned in my tiny way at the Rock Garden, was a very valuable resource to draw on.

Other frictions came from the clash between Vince Clarke and Martin Gore. They were pulling the band in opposite directions: Vince wanted a very different sound from Martin, and up to this point they had held together through mutual admiration and a group determination to succeed. They were all kids from working-class Basildon, all destined for the factory or the dole if music failed them.

We never supported Depeche Mode again and lost contact with them as a band. A few months after the Venue gig, I heard a day or two before it hit the *NME* that Vince had left Depeche Mode and was forming a two-piece called Yazoo with a girl he had met called Alison Moyet. Of the four members of Depeche Mode it was Vince Clarke who I had clicked with, and it would be this relationship that would take Jan and me to the next stage of our careers.

13

We too entered a series of group convulsions immediately after the Venue gig. After much agonising we decided to change the line-up and to take on a drummer. The decision was talked through during many an evening rehearsal at the flat. The advantages were clear; our pitter-patter drum machine just wasn't up to scratch and we had no money to buy the sort of sound Depeche Mode could afford. After all we had said and thought about drummers vs. drum machines we realised that, for live work at least, we would have to have a human with sticks.

We auditioned in a tiny rehearsal room at the back of a shop near Southend High Street and finally settled on a guy called Colin McGlone, who we had seen play at a truly hideous club called Zero 6. He had been in a fantastic, recently defunct band called Newspeak. Colin was tight, had a good musical ear and, most importantly, he understood what we were trying to do.

With this line-up the gigs started to come thick and fast, and we were beginning to build a good fan base. But we all knew that recording was the real key to the future, and we spent anything we made from playing live on recording our latest material. In this way we met an interesting array of musicians. There were the old rockers, the forty-somethings who had been in Dr Feelgood and other R & B bands as well as ageing rock 'n' roll artists like Marty Wilde. Many of these guys ran their own studios which were dotted over Essex, often in remote farmhouses or behind industrial units on Canvey Island estates. Most of them had zero empathy with what we were doing and we simply paid our two or three hundred quid for a day and a night session and left with our new tape of three or four songs. These were duly sent to any record company we could think of and 100 times out of 100 we heard nothing back, meaning we had to write off more money on lost cassettes and postage as well as accepting more huge dents to our pride.

And what had happened to Greg/Yvette? The compilation album did appear, selling about seven copies, six of them behind the Iron Curtain, but it was wonderful to have a record with your name on it. It took pride of place in our record collection and we scrounged enough money to buy a few hundred copies between us to sell at gigs, so the sales figures gradually rose from seven to perhaps two hundred and seven during the following year.

We stayed in touch with Greg, knowing that although he wasn't big time he might be a useful contact one day if we happened to record an obvious smash. Besides, we liked him. He was unreliable and sometimes self-important but he could also be funny and generous and it was nice to believe the flattering things he would occasionally say about us.

About six months into the new line-up we were really on a roll. By March 1982, we had an average of two gigs lined up a week for the following few months, we were appearing in the local paper on a regular basis and even playing live on our local radio station. Then, early in May, we made the definitive Watch With Mother recording which, it is now obvious, was a missing link that pulled together the disparate threads that led Jan and I to the real pop world and beyond.

Jan had written the lyrics to a song called 'When Sex Was Fun', which dealt with how some people grow disillusioned with their relationship. In retrospect, I should have taken its lyrics to be something of an omen or at least a signal that all was not well . . . but no. Although lyrics can be interpreted in all sorts of ways and the best can apply to many different situations, they often spring from some genuine feeling in the writer. But the true meaning of what Jan was trying to articulate did not become apparent until later.

Jan's lyrics and vocal melody for 'When Sex Was Fun' fitted perfectly some music I had been playing around with for a while, a choppy guitar-based song, up-tempo and with a catchy riff for the chorus. Jan and I got together to construct the song one evening and it all fell into place so easily we just knew it was going to be special. We played it to Martin and Colin at our next rehearsal and in ten minutes the song was almost whole, it just worked so well.

As luck would have it, we had arranged a recording session at a London studio for the following week and as we talked about recording 'When Sex Was Fun' and dropping one of the other songs we had thought we would use, Martin started jumping up and down excitedly and saying that he had a fantastic idea. 'I have a friend at college who plays trombone and he's in the brass section for Crab, the Brighton band? Why don't we get them to play on the song?'

It was an inspired idea. We met the guys for the first time the day of the recording. They turned up in the afternoon after we had laid down the basic tracks of guitar, bass, drums and guide vocal and they just played the most fantastic horn arrangement, which completely transformed what was already a good song into a great one.

'When Sex Was Fun' and another track, 'Bikini Trauma', were finished in one day and when we got the tape home we realised they were a million times better than anything we had done before. The problem was the perennial one – what should we do with these songs now? The constant round of sending tapes to A & R departments, traipsing along to fruit-less, usually humiliating meetings and spending our precious college grants on phone calls to London trying to persuade A & R men to come to our next gig was beginning to wear us down. Greg liked the tape, but had no plans for another compilation and didn't think 'When Sex Was Fun' was a strong single, even though we totally disagreed. He promised to talk to a few people, but nothing happened.

Then, one day a few weeks before my finals, as I walked down the steps of Temple underground station and on to the platform, I had the most inspired idea of my entire life. I remember the exact moment with amazing clarity. I had been in a desperate mood, weighed down with the effort of trying to balance the band with my college work and utterly convinced I was heading for abject failure in both simultaneously. I had left King's and walked towards the tube station racking my brains for a way in which I could turn everything round with a single grand gesture. I entered the tube station, flashed my pass, took the steps three at a time, and, as I arrived on the platform and the train pulled into the station, the idea arrived whole, a complete entity, simple, beautiful.

It was this. We had three things going for us: 1) A great song with 'When Sex Was Fun'; 2) we had remained friends with Vince Clarke; 3) we had Greg and his little record label. Why not put them all together?

By the time I stepped off the tube at Fenchurch Street to catch the train to Leigh, the details were falling into place.

Jan and I would go to see Vince and ask him to contribute a
song to an EP (extended play) and we would put 'When Sex
Was Fun' and 'Bikini Trauma' with it and perhaps get in
another band to complete the line-up. The record would be
put out by Greg's label and would be a hit because of Yazoo,
but we might get noticed at the same time. I realised that to
complete the plan we would have to do the record for a
charity or a cause so that Vince wouldn't think we were
exploiting his success. It was perfect, and I could hardly
contain myself during the hour-long journey to Leigh and
the waiting telephone.

14

Before we could take the idea to Vince Clarke, we had to come up with a charity for the project. We wanted to support something we all cared about and knew Vince would go for as well. It was now the spring of 1982, the Greenham Common protestors were in the news, Jan and I had been on two marches already that year, including an amazing event that had attracted over 100,000 people to a rally in Hyde Park, and we had met a few people involved with CND. A new force on the live circuit at that time was an organisation called No Nukes Music, which held concerts around the country in an attempt to raise awareness among rock fans and money for CND. We knew from chats in the pub with Vince that he and Depeche Mode were pro-disarmament and all of us in Watch With Mother were too. No Nukes Music seemed the perfect choice.

As soon as Jan and I had settled upon this, I called Vince.

He was pleased to hear from us. I told him we had an idea we wanted to put to him, and asked if we could meet up. The next day we found ourselves outside the door of Vince Clarke's new flat in Basildon.

Things had changed for him in the months since he had left Depeche Mode. The first royalties from his hits with the band had come through and he had bought a modest flat close to where he had grown up and only a few hundred yards from where his erstwhile colleagues had lived and where their parents still lived and worked. He shared the flat with his girlfriend, Deb, and seemed to be far happier than when we had last seen him a few days after the gig at The Venue. He had been working hard, he told us, and had just finished the first mix of the new album he had recorded with Alison Moyet, *Upstairs at Eric's*, a record that would, a few months later, be perched at Number 1 in the album charts.

Deb made us a cup of tea and we sat in their large but spartan sitting room. They had only just moved in and still had ornaments packed in boxes, there were no pictures up and the walls were unpainted plaster. The only things in the sitting room were a couple of leather sofas and a vast and very expensive-looking stereo system.

We chatted about what we had been doing and he told us about the new arrangement with the girl he called Alf, what a great singer she was and how he had discovered her after auditioning about a hundred prospective vocalists. Then he amazed us by playing the white label (the first pressing) of what would be their debut single, 'Only You'.

From the opening sounds to the last drum beat it sounded wonderful, and Alf's was simply the best female voice I had heard in pop music. The production was of course superb, and the tightness and economy of the music amazed me. I remember Jan saying with complete sincerity that she thought it would fail as a single because it was far too good for the charts. Fortunately for Vince, she was as wrong as anyone could have been – 'Only You' went straight to Number 1 a couple of weeks later and stayed there for three weeks.

And so I eventually got around to asking the big question. I explained my idea, told him we would like to do the record for CND and that I had a contact there. I explained about Greg's label and the idea of an EP and wondered if he would be interested in offering a re-mix of a song or perhaps a track left over from the recording of the album, even a B-side.

Vince was great, he didn't hesitate in saying that, in principle, he would be delighted to be involved. He said he'd have to pass it by Alf and get his record company and publishers to sanction the licensing of the song, but that that should not present a major problem. He asked us what we were planning to put on the record and we told him about the new songs we had recorded, but although I had the tape in my pocket and had arrived with every intention of playing it, after hearing 'Only You' I'm afraid I didn't have the guts to, and pretended I had left the tape at home. Months later, when the record was made and our two songs were placed alongside Yazoo's contribution, 'Goodbye '70s', they sounded okay and Vince later told me he really liked them, which prompted me to confess that I could have played the songs that day in his flat but had bottled out.

That night we called Greg and told him about our idea. He went for it straight away, which was no big surprise: Vince was very hot at the time and everyone was itching to hear what his new material would sound like. Privileged to be among the first dozen or so people to hear the debut Yazoo single, we assured Greg that Vince's new band were much better than Depeche Mode and that he would soon be even more famous than he already was. Greg said he would talk to a few people but our plan sounded very promising.

Now we were beginning to get really excited about the whole thing, but there remained one more link in the chain.

The same evening I called No Nukes Music and arranged to go along to their offices. And so, two days later, immediately after taking my final Organic Chemistry exam, I headed off to the offices of No Nukes Music which was in a back room in a decrepit building off the Charing Cross Road.

In itself, the meeting was pretty uneventful. The guy who ran the outfit was an old hippie who was grateful for our support and enthusiastic enough about our offer of giving the entire proceeds from the record to their cause, but he had obviously never heard of Vince Clarke or Depeche Mode and I was beginning to think that perhaps I was barking up the wrong tree. But then it occurred to me that what this well-intentioned bloke thought about the music we or Vince were making was totally irrelevant. We wanted to give money to CND and he was the best route to them, and besides, the fact that a very famous pop star was going to be behind it meant that it would sell well without any support from No Nukes Music.

So, slightly miffed, but pleased to have settled that side of the project, I turned to leave his office, and as I walked out, I passed a low-lying table covered with papers, leaflets and general detritus. Looking down, I saw something that, combined with my reason for being there that day, turned out to be a 'something' that would change my life.

The something was a piece of paper. Written on it was: 'John Hade, Thompson Twins manager', followed by an address. While the old hippie was looking away, I scribbled the number on to the back of my cheque book and left the building.

15

Looking back, everything seemed to move very, very quickly after that, but to us at the time it felt as though things were happening at a snail's pace.

At first we did nothing with John Hade's address. In fact, the cheque book was almost finished, and a few days later I threw it into a kitchen drawer and forgot about it. I like to think I was just being cool, that John Hade was just one of many contacts we had at the time, but it was more to do with the fact that my finals were looming and the band had a string of gigs lined up.

The band had also undergone further changes. Perhaps influenced by Vince and Alison, Jan and I decided one evening to radically overhaul the way we were doing things . . . again. By this time, Martin was drifting away and concentrating on his own university career, and Colin was playing in other bands as well as with us. But more importantly, Jan and I wanted to be seen as a two-piece. It is clear with hindsight we were following a trend set by other far more successful musicians. The Eurythmics were just breaking through and there was Yazoo of course. There was nothing original about our decision but it did seem like the right thing to do – it was neater, more efficient and, crucially, more fashionable.

So, a week before the cover and labels for the EP were produced, we talked to Martin and Colin and told them that we would be changing our name to Colour-Me-Pop (after another '60s TV show), that for promotional purposes we would be a two-piece but if they were agreeable we would all still play live together. Amazingly, they were quite happy to go along with this. As a consequence, the songs on the EP were by Colour-Me-Pop but credited to all four of us, Jan and I had some promo pictures done and the baby's face was discarded along with any further plans for lyrics about indoctrination.

This was actually a very good time to initiate new ideas and to change, because the process of turning our concept for an EP into vinyl took months. Vince kept his promise and his record company passed on to Greg a tape of 'Goodbye '70s', a song written by Alf, and we gave him our master tape of 'When Sex Was Fun' and 'Bikini Trauma'. The final two songs for the record came from a band called Sudeten Creche, who turned out to be Greg's brother, Paul, and a friend of his who had recently recorded two songs which Greg decided would be perfect to complete the project. The entire ensemble was an odd blend, ranging from the electro-pop of Yazoo through the rather jazzy/New Wave sound of our songs to the gentle balladry of Paul Carlin, a.k.a. Sudeten Creche. And as Greg played his part – cutting the master disc, organising the legal side of things with Mute Records and paying for everything, we got on with our schizo-roles of playing both pop stars and students.

We were naturally very excited by the thought that we may have made our breakthrough record, but we had to get on with our lives as if nothing was happening. The gigs we played at that time all merge into one, and I find it difficult to remember when each one took place, where it was or how it went.

One that stands out was a gig we played at a sprawling stately home deep in the Essex countryside one Saturday night. Excited by the prospect of a hoped-for rider of tender duckling sandwiches, our own spit roast and perhaps a crate of Cristal, we were rather disappointed to find ourselves booked on a heavy-metal night and to discover that our dressing room had once been the outside loo for the servants. But all was not lost: the organisers had thoughtfully placed for us a four-pack of cheap lager in the changing-room-cum-toilet.

After a microsecond surveying the leather-clad audience and the first band on stage, we made a collective unspoken decision to get thoroughly plastered at the bar. We had a friend driving for us that night who was being paid not to drink, and so we thought we could let ourselves go. The gig flew by and the hostility of the audience, which grew from about the third bar of our opening number, simply washed over us. We just let rip, producing what, ten years later, might have been termed thrash-metal versions of New Wave/electro-pop songs. I wish I'd taped it – we might have been on to something. But the organisers asked us to stop after four songs, which was fine by us.

Three-quarters pissed, I decided to join the audience for the between-bands disco. In my inebriated state I was uncharacteristically chatty with the gaggle of young guys dancing wildly to 'Paranoia' and 'Smoke On The Water', and perhaps they failed to recognise me because they accepted me flailing away in my ripped mac, DMs and eye make-up. But then rather stupidly, I now realise, I shouted over the noise into the ear of one particularly beefy specimen that his air guitar was out of tune. First came a blank look, then a startled, rabbit-caught-by-headlights bewilderment before his face fell into half-smile. To my enduring relief, this barn of a man laughed, a boom that broke through the barrage of metal and he bashed me on the back with his giant's paw.

After that I decided to get out while the going was good and found Martin at the bar. We both agreed things were a little uncomfortable and could turn nasty. The next thing I knew I was outside on the vast, empty gravel driveway, leaving behind the thud-thud-thud of some Suzi Quatro number and stumbling towards the sixteen-year-old VW Beetle in which we then all travelled to and from gigs. Jan was already by the car with the guitars and our synthesiser half in the boot.

It was incredibly cold and my head hurt. A dense fog had descended upon the place, making it look like the set of a Hammer horror movie. That part of Essex is notorious for the pea-souper fogs that wash in from the coast and wrap everything so tightly you can hardly see your own outstretched hands. This was one such fog and the moist freezing air sobered me up instantly. I slammed shut the boot and jumped into the passenger seat as Martin and Jan piled into the back. Dave took the wheel, revved up and we sped out through the gates and into the winding lane beyond.

Five yards from the house and it had disappeared in the all-consuming fog. Suddenly we found ourselves completely enshrouded. The under-powered lights of the Beetle (Noddy's 'other' car) meant we had to crawl along at about 10 mph, slowing even more for the frequent bends. And it grew worse – in fact it became so bad we had to take turns walking in front of the car, guiding it along the lane like something out of a Charlie Chaplin film.

*

The first time we played as Colour-Me-Pop was at the Grand Hotel in Leigh, a short walk from our flat. We had prepared a special light show for the evening and had made a Super-8 film, a sort of psychedelic mish-mash of ideas which was projected on to a make-shift screen behind us, *à la* Velvet Underground circa 1966. It was a very exciting evening, we played well, and the audience, made up largely of the loyal fans who had stuck with us for at least the past year, were on particularly good form, and as usual 'Psycho Killer' brought the house down.

Obviously our tiny following loved us, but somehow, somewhere along the line we had also generated surprising hostility among the semi-pro community in Southend. Several times after the gig people we had considered friends quite deliberately snubbed us. Although we had said nothing, word had got out about the EP and suddenly it appeared that because we'd had the temerity to find ourselves on the edge of success, we were not the same people we had once been. Suddenly we had to be knocked, brought down to size; such is life in the semi-pro music scene. Today, it's called the Poppy Syndrome, but the ironic thing is that we'd hardly gestated.

It had been nothing overt, no punch-ups in the gents, just snide remarks from people who had been frequent visitors at the flat, sarcastic remarks about soon being on *Top of the Pops* from those who had once lent us equipment or helped us set up the gear on stage. Jan took it the right way, seeing such comments as compliments, but me, being me, I became instantly morose. I remember ensuring the equipment was safely stowed in the car before telling the others I needed some air, then I slipped away and walked down to the beach a few hundred yards from the Grand Hotel to sit on the shingle and cast stones into the estuary, wondering what might lay ahead. Were those people at the gig right? Was I stepping beyond myself and playing the pop star without really having done anything? Or were they simply jealous? And what of my reaction? Why was I now so upset? If they were right and we were stepping into the fast lane, then I would have to learn to live with far worse criticism. And for a second I wondered whether this was really what I wanted . . . But only for a second.

16

We finally saw the object of our dreams, the EP entitled
Europe in the Year Zero, in June 1982, some two months after
we had first approached Greg with the whole package. And it
was a glorious moment.

For the cover, Greg had chosen a grainy black and white
photograph of a TV anchor woman reading the news.
Apparently, she was from an East German station; she looked
ageless with amazingly prominent cheekbones and huge eyes
and had been chosen, we heard, because Greg fancied her.
We were glad the cover kept away from images of the Cold
War or nuclear holocaust and thought Greg had got it just
right. We picked up our box of twenty-five records from his
Fulham office and brought them home on the train. Colin
and Martin met us at the flat and I placed the precious disc
on the turntable. Knowing the landlady was out, I cranked
up the volume.

For some odd reason, this piece of vinyl sounded so much better than the tape. It was exactly the same of course, but I suppose it was a little like drinking an average wine from a crystal glass. The mere fact we were listening to our music on the same format in which we listened to professional groups rather than on a cassette (which almost anyone could do) made it very special.

We had no idea what was going to happen next with the EP, and in a way, I liked that. Up to this point I had always been the one doing almost everything, promoting us and selling our wares. It was disquieting to let someone else do the pushing, but it was also a relief and I had to simply trust that Greg and his company (now re-named Sexual Phonograph) would 'do the business'.

Nothing much happened at first. We did our bit, promoting the record at gigs and giving copies to local journalists, radio DJs and venue managers, but we all knew that if it was to stand a chance then Greg's efforts would be the thing that counted.

The day after we picked up our copies, Alison Moyet called to ask if she could collect hers and Vince's. We had arranged a couple of boxes for them when we visited Greg and had them on the sitting-room floor of the flat. Alf turned up that evening. Shy almost to the point of invisibility, she smiled briefly and mumbled a 'hello', declined a cup of tea and just picked up the records and turned back to the door. Maybe she had a car waiting, but I couldn't believe she was so quiet and obviously uncomfortable, and it reinforced the idea that so many pop stars who have more than enough confidence to get up on stage and wiggle their arses, often find it hard to string two words together in company. So that was Alf; great singer, but not exactly Ronald McDonald.

We really shouldn't have worried about the EP. It now seems obvious the record was going to work, the songs were good, contemporary and well produced and of course the presence of Yazoo ensured it would be noticed.

The first thing to happen was a play on John Peel. Although the John Peel show was renowned for playing the most obscure music around, there can be few greater thrills than hearing your record played on Radio 1 and my memory of that moment is absolutely vivid. And John Peel liked us so much he played our tracks several more times during the next few weeks. And then, a day after our first Radio 1 play, we got our first reviews in both the *NME* and *Melody Maker*.

Melody Maker said: '"When Sex Was Fun" and "Bikini Trauma" show plenty of promise. What they lack in production and presence they make up for with a brave lean towards jazzy pop.' *NME* called us 'earthy', whatever that meant, and a local paper defined 'When Sex Was Fun' as 'jaunty and quirky', while 'Bikini Trauma' was 'unsettling, dreamy and Bohemian'. At the same time, Jan and I began to get some attention in a variety of pop papers and magazines. We had produced a really cool package of photos and a press release to launch Colour-Me-Pop and the record was obviously a great support for that.

Then one hot Thursday (the day the *NME* appeared each week), I went to the corner newsagent, studied the paper avidly for any mention of us or the record and, feeling a little deflated by the total absence of anything linked to us or it, I reached the back of the paper, and found the Indie Singles Chart, and there it was.

Admittedly, the record was perched at Number 49 in the Top 50, but it was there, and I felt the hairs on the back of my neck stand up.

It was a humble start, but it proved to be just the beginning for *Europe in the Year Zero*. From Number 49 the record rose through Number 46 to 22 before peaking after a few weeks at Number 7. We were off the block.

A few days after the record entered the chart, Greg called to say it had sold an amazing 15,000 copies. But that very afternoon there was even more excitement. We had a call from a Radio 1 plugger.

For those unaware of the existence of such beings, radio pluggers are there simply to convince top DJs to play certain records. There have been accusations over the years that some unscrupulous characters within the industry have bribed certain DJs to play certain records, but these are absolutely, most definitely, without any shadow of a doubt scurrilous, scabrous, horrid lies. As you enter the stratospheric world of recording artists, one of the things you learn about pluggers is that they are as honest and trustworthy as A & R men.

Our plugger called us on a car phone. And to us in 1982 this was an incredible revelation. He was obviously a serious and highly successful plugger, a plugger of the first rank, a king among pluggers, because in 1982 only billionaires had car phones. He wanted to know if anyone else was promoting the EP and we gave him Greg's number.

Immensely excited, we went out for a long walk and talked about how we could really make it with a plugger behind us. We had a chart position, a great deal of experience, a nice promotional package and, most importantly perhaps, a collection of new material which just the two of us had recorded and with which we felt really confident, knowing a couple of the songs had singles potential. As we returned to the flat, we heard the phone ringing, dashed in and heard Greg's voice on the line.

After all the excitement it was hard to take the big letdown. Somewhere between concept and release, it had been decided by Yazoo's record label, Mute, that the EP would have to be a limited edition, and the cap on the sales was, naturally, 15,000 copies. As a consequence, our plugger would have nothing to plug because Sexual Phonograph could not press or sell any more copies. Greg explained this as gently as he could, even though he was quite naturally aggrieved – he would liked to have sold ten times as many of the thing too. Even so, it hurt, and as I put the phone down I felt the whiff of sudden success drift out through the still open front door of the flat.

But as we recoiled from learning there would be a strict limit to the potential of our EP, it was already quietly weaving its way into the consciousness of the music business and planting seeds in many unexpected places. And other things slipped into place too. Soon after we had received our box of records I had remembered the cheque book and John Hade's address and had sent him a copy, along with a letter explaining who we were and what we were trying to achieve. We didn't know it at the time, but the very day we received news about the limits placed on the EP he was playing it to his business partners in London.

17

As *Europe in the Year Zero* began to percolate through the pop world other aspects of our lives also began to take some decidedly weird turns. Just as success seemed within our grasp, my relationship with Jan was beginning to fall apart.

I still cannot say precisely why this was happening; I didn't understand it then and I still don't now. I guess we were just drifting in opposite directions. Very little was said; perhaps that was the problem, but as the EP made the indie chart and our careers began to happen, Jan felt the need to express her feelings.

She had become involved with a couple of people during our time together. The previous summer there had been a seventeen-year-old German student she had been attracted to. She had been teaching English to foreign students during the summer vacation and about twenty minutes into the course she had fallen for a spindly youth called Heinrich or

Karlheinz or some such Teutonic moniker. Then, after knowing him two days, she had managed to pilfer his virginity on the cliffs overlooking Southend pier. I only found out about it after the Germans had returned home.

Then there was Dave Smith, a Marxist philosophy graduate about fifteen years older than Jan whom she had met while working in a supermarket during a college holiday. A few months later there had been another brief encounter, this time with a mystery student from Cambridge whom she had met on a weekend field-trip studying frogspawn or something similarly appropriate. Clearly, Jan did not have a 'type'.

Combined with these dalliances, Jan had always carried a torch for the boy who had deflowered her, a friend of mine from schooldays called Simon. Simon had taken the hippie trail to India and then lived in the States for a time. At irregular intervals he would reappear in England looking weirdly different each time. About six months earlier he had arrived at the flat and we stayed up late into the night smoking dope and drinking the gut-rot Spanish wine he had brought back from his latest trip. About one o'clock in the morning I went to bed and left them talking. Waking an hour later, I wandered into the sitting room to find them snogging on the sofa. I turned on my heel and two minutes later Jan was in bed trying to talk me down and Simon had left.

It was odd how we had survived these infidelities and even odder that I never reciprocated. I suppose it is obvious I needed her more than she needed me, but by the day of Greg's call we had hit a serious low. Perhaps it was simply the shock of realising the roller-coaster ride we thought we were on might turn out to be a spin on the tea-cup carousel after all.

Jan and I went for a walk along the beach and the whole lot came out – her feelings of entrapment and frustration, her anxieties about our future both as a couple and in terms of our careers. Somehow my own fears mutated into bitterness and anger. I hated her for her lack of faith in us, in me, and I felt resentful she had contributed so little to the band, to us. Soon, we found ourselves yelling at each other, scaring the shit out of the seagulls and a group of pensioners taking their constitutionals along the prom. I stormed off home, leaving Jan in tears on the beach. Once in the flat I found my railcard and headed for the station and the next train to college.

The confluence of events was astonishing. There I was with a record in the indie chart, I was perilously close to ending a seven-year relationship with my girlfriend, and that same afternoon I was due to be in college to collect my degree results. It was almost too much to take. But then things got even worse.

Because I was spending most of my life in a dream world where the only points of contact were the *NME* and my guitar, I had heard nothing of the bus and underground strike called for that day, an event that had effectively paralysed the city, and it was only as I emerged into Fenchurch Street Station that I saw a large blackboard with the announcement of strike action emblazoned in chalk capitals. Then it began to rain – no summer shower but a full-on monsoon. And so I walked.

Arriving at college, drenched, everyone had been and gone and I found myself alone before the noticeboard with the exam results pinned to it in long rows of pages covered in tiny type. I knew I had passed, but it was great to see it in black and white, and as I walked away momentarily triumphant, I thanked my lucky stars there had not been a few more gigs the week of my finals.

I went to the bar but could find no one I knew there. I desperately needed to be with people, I could feel myself being ripped apart by too many conflicting emotions. How do you deal with success and failure simultaneously? I had no idea then, but during the course of the following six months these twinned feelings would become familiar accomplices.

Despondent and not knowing what to do next, I headed for the exit on the Strand and rather wistfully stopped at the student pigeonholes. 'W' was filled with leaflets and circulars and notes for all the others who shared the same first letter of my surname, and I almost overlooked a scrap of paper folded in four with my name pencilled hurriedly across it.

I opened it and found a message from a couple of college friends, Nigel and Oliver. 'Gotta spare ticket for the Gang of Four, the Palais, tonight – wanna meet us there? 7.30, by the doors?' Clearly three years at King's had done wonders for their grammar.

I looked at my watch; it was 5.30. Even walking, I could make it in time and I loved the Gang of Four. I headed through the door on to the rush-hour Strand just in time to see one of my fellow nouveau graduates dropping his trousers and giving the traffic a celebratory moony. Turning the other way I headed off towards Hammersmith.

Nigel and Oliver were outside the main doors and just about to go in because I was so late. They looked an odd pair, a cyberpunk Laurel and Hardy, Nigel short and skinny, Oliver tall and fat. They were both wearing ripped macs and calf-length Doc Marten's, Nigel had on a white collarless shirt with the frayed French cuffs hanging six inches beyond the sleeves of his coat, and Oliver wore a sweaty T-shirt carrying a foot-long picture of a tampon.

The gig was just amazing, almost matching the Talking Heads concert at the Hammersmith Odeon I had had the great privilege to attend in 1980 when an unknown Irish band called U2 had been third on the bill and blown the roof off. The Gang of Four had an absolutely unique sound, blending punk with funk. It was incredibly powerful music which, if you let it, could completely possess you. And that night I was open to a little possession.

The three of us headed for the bar and stayed there until the band appeared, then, already half-cut, I forced a way to the front and danced wildly for two hours hardly pausing to breathe. I remember the heat was almost overwhelming and the volume was cranked up so that you could feel the bass notes thumping into your chest. The guitarist, Andrew Gill, was one of my musical heroes, a quite astonishing musician who had a totally unique sound. He managed to get notes out of his instrument I never knew existed until he played them – an '80s Hendrix if ever there was one. And the moment that remains clearest in my mind came during the encore. The band had settled into an amazing funk groove and Gill came crashing in over the top with the most distorted yet melodic solo I'd ever heard, then he turned, picked up a full can of beer from where it had been standing on an amp and started rubbing it on the strings with his right hand as he played a huge cascade of notes with his left. The beer surged up in the can and flowed all over the guitar and in great streams into the air as the music reached an orgiastic high.

We could hardly hear each other speak as we left the show, our clothes sopping wet with sweat. The chill of the night hit us within seconds. I had no idea where we were going, I had made no plans, I had cut myself adrift and it only felt all right because I was drunk. I just let the others take the lead; it was what I needed to do after so long trying to control things, trying to hold together my relationship, holding together my college life, trying to make it.

Oliver had stayed fairly sober and had brought his car. Nigel knew of a party in Brixton at a student house shared by a group of medics. The journey south was a haze, but at least it was warm in the car and gradually the ringing in my ears subsided. Over the river the traffic cleared and soon we were heading through Clapham and on to Brixton.

In 1982, Brixton was almost a no-go area for middle-class

white boys like me. The riots of the previous year had invaded the social consciousness and the place possessed an aura akin to Harlem. You just didn't go there. But students and musicians hardly counted, and we seemed to possess no fear. This could be because we looked so poor and had little concern for muggers. Nigel, however, had a penchant for taking things just that little bit too far, and suggested we score some dope on the way to the party. And so I found myself at midnight, twelve hours after leaving Jan on the beach fifty miles away, waiting in a side-street in Brixton in an old Mini looking out across a darkened street to what can only be described as a war zone where Nigel 'knew someone'.

The party was packed. We had sobered up and those crammed into the house like, well, sardines on an over-booked sardine charter flight to Sardinia were almost all drunk. And in the early '80s, booze was the drug of choice for all the medics we knew, so that when Nigel mentioned we had some gear, we were shown a room at the top of the house where we could lock ourselves away and not disturb the sensibilities of the others.

I was beginning to get depressed, I was sober again and feeling bad about leaving the flat without telling Jan where I had gone, but then Nigel rolled up a huge spliff and before long I began to forget a little. But even then I didn't feel quite right. Often cannabis has the effect of heightening one's emotions, so that if you feel happy it makes you feel happier and sometimes when you're down it takes you further that way. I became no more depressed, just uncomfortable. Slightly paranoid, I imagined the others were judging me, wondering who I thought I was, thinking I had pretensions of fame. As far as I know, no one was thinking this at all, but I had an edgy memory of a party not unlike this one from about a year earlier. I had been introduced to a tall, good-looking guy with bleached spiky hair who simply exuded confidence and self-respect. He had told me he was

recording in London, and thinking he was at a place not dis-
similar to Crazy Sound, I was shattered when he casually
remarked that his band were at Sarm West, possibly the best
studio in the world. It turned out he was the bassist with
ABC and they were in the middle of recording *Lexicon of
Love*, one of the great '80s albums. In retrospect, I can see
why he came across as confident.

Later, as I smoked more, the haze returned and I was once
again happy to be led rather than having to think about
where I was or what I was doing. I have no recollection of
leaving the party or of travelling anywhere, but I remember
waking up on the floor in a darkened room, sitting up suddenly and seeing Oliver slumped in a chair reading a book
and drinking coffee. Behind him a crack of light seeped
through a heavy velvet curtain and I knew it was daytime
again. We were in a flat in Battersea owned by Oliver's parents. Nigel lay on the floor next to me, snoring.

Thankfully, the transport strike was over, and blinking at
the painful, thrusting rays of the sun, my mouth dry and
harbouring the rancid taste of stale beer and tobacco, I
descended into the cool, comforting darkness of the underground and back east to Fenchurch Street and the train to
Leigh.

The flat was empty, and I had the definite feeling no one
had been there the previous night. It was warm. I drew the
curtains and opened a window letting in the sea breeze and
the sound of traffic from the road. It was only then I noticed
a note on the table. For a moment I thought Jan had gone,
that this was it, it was all over, that everything, our relationship, our career, our past, our present, our future had all
dissolved. But it was not a farewell note. It contained a single
stunning sentence: 'John Hade called. He wants to meet us.'

18

John Hade was smaller than I had imagined he would be but also far more open and friendly. He looked too straight to be a musician but too rock 'n' roll for a businessman; which, for the Thompson Twins, was just right, I reasoned. In this way he appeared to be cool but also carried authority: neither Spinal Tap's Ian Faith nor Brian Epstein. In another incarnation, he would perhaps have liked to have been Malcolm McLaren, but then again, at the time we met him, he seemed pretty excited about being John Hade. And with good reason. He had been with the earliest version of the band when they had formed in Chesterfield in 1977. He had promoted their earliest singles on their own label and had moved with them to London in 1980, when they had given up their day jobs and taken the enormous leap of trying to make a living from music. Now, in the early summer of 1982, they were on the verge of huge success, and John knew it.

Jan and I were already Thompson Twins fans when we met John. We had seen the band on *The Old Grey Whistle Test* the previous Christmas and were impressed by their unique sound, a blend of ethnic rhythms and quirky guitar and vocals. You could hear their influences, from Talking Heads and the leftovers of the New Wave scene, but they had fused it all in a refreshing way. Early in the New Year, Jan and I had gone straight out to get anything we could find by the Thompson Twins.

The original band had been a four-piece – Tom Bailey (bass), Chris Bell (drums), John Roog (guitar) and Pete Dodd (vocals and guitar) – and they had changed line-up several times after moving to London, where they all lived in a legalised squat in Clapham with John Hade occupying another run-down building across the road. They had taken on a roadie, Joe Leeway, who later became an official member of the band and played percussion. Some time later Tom had met a New Zealander, Alannah Currie, who had been in an all-girl band called The Unfuckables. Over the course of several singles and two albums, *A Product of . . .* in 1981 and *Set* in early 1982, they had begun to emerge as an important force on the alternative music scene, variously defined by the music press as 'cult' and 'fringe'.

And this had really been their problem. The original Thompson Twins had a great sound, but one that would never appeal to a large audience; it was just too eclectic. They also had an image problem. By the time of *Set*, Tom Bailey had begun to be seen as the frontman, but he hadn't really developed any identity as a lead singer. I remember in October 1982, we were sitting in the kitchen of his house during a break in the tour, as he poured water into the teapot, Tom noticed me looking bemused at a photograph of a guy with dreadlocks playing bass on some stage somewhere. 'That was me during my dreadlocked, hippie, bass-playing incarnation,' he said with a laugh.

But just before Jan and I met up with John Hade, the idea that the band could continue as a group of dreadlocked, hippies was no longer good enough. Between us seeing them on *The Old Grey Whistle Test* and meeting their manager, the band had completely transformed themselves.

The first surprise came when John told us we would not be able to meet the band because they were finishing tracks for their new album in a studio in the Caribbean. And by the way John told us this so matter-of-factly, we knew immediately everything had changed. But what, we wondered, had taken the Thompson Twins from Clapham to a sun-drenched mixing desk?

The first half of 1982 had been a time of great upheaval for the Thompson Twins. Their second album had done better than their first, but had not come remotely close to setting the world alight; in fact, with sales of a few thousand, in some respects it must have felt like a wasted effort. They had used a top producer – Steve Lillywhite – they had recorded in a great studio and had done everything right, or so they had thought.

But then other forces began to impact upon them. At about the time the album stalled, Tom and John had become interested in EST, an organisation that believed the individual could focus his or her mind, ambitions and desires toward success in any form they wished. EST promoted a set of strict processes by which personal growth and development could be achieved, and although neither Tom nor John ever became obsessive devotees, they learned a few tricks from it.

Fundamental to the changes was their realisation that the original Thompson Twins had been a great musical unit but that they only appealed to a few people. And as Tom and John, and later Alannah and Joe, began to change their way of thinking, they started to realise that if they were to succeed as musicians they would have to make major changes to their approach to making and marketing music.

Other factors were at work simultaneously. The band were touring constantly, pouring enormous but largely wasted effort into trying to promote themselves, but the foundations of what they were doing were not right for the time. The music scene was changing rapidly and their sound, although original, was slipping still further out of sync with modern pop sensibilities. A few of those in the know within the music world were able to see this before the Twins themselves and some tried to encourage a change.

Early in 1982 Ian Pye, the then editor of *NME*, had had a long chat with Tom after a gig in Newcastle under Lyme and quizzed him about whether he really needed all the musicians who trooped around with him. This, Ian now thinks, may have nudged him further into thinking about overhauling their career.

But the biggest change came not from shifts in ideology, the influence of journalists or even the flow of fashion, but from a single song, one of the tracks written by Tom and tucked away on *Set* entitled 'In The Name Of Love'.

Early in 1982, this track was seen by the band as just another on the album. It had a great rhythm, a neat lyric at once universal and personal, and some catchy tunes bouncing around in the mix. But the version on *Set* sounded much like any other Thompson Twins song, percussive, upbeat and ethnic, full of guitars and bongos; but Tom, who had always been the really imaginative musical force within the band, realised the song had hidden potential.

One evening, after the album was mixed and finished, he returned alone to the studio and remixed an entirely different version of 'In The Name Of Love'. He added more synth parts and took the guitars and 'natural' instruments lower in the mix, and as he emerged from the studio in the early hours, he knew he had done something that would radically change the course of his life and the lives of those in the band.

At first he didn't know what to do with the remix, but eventually he played it to John and Alannah. To his relief, they got it immediately. Encouraged, he played it to the other members of the band.

They hated it. This sound was simply not the direction they wanted to head in, they had planned to continue with the eclectic mix of their first two albums and believed music should be live and that guitars were superior to synthesisers. But most importantly, they hated the new synthetic pop of Tom's version of a song they had been happy with already.

Fortunately, the Thompson Twins' management and publishing company saw things Tom's way. But even more crucially, a couple of DJs in New York liked the song and played it constantly on their local radio stations. Before long, word spread; 'In The Name Of Love' became a smash in the clubs of New York and a hit on the dance scene throughout America. By the spring of 1982, the new sound of the Thompson Twins was top of the Billboard dance chart and the band had their first sniff of commercial success.

Of course, a split was inevitable, and by this time Tom and John were ready for it. As soon as Tom had had his remix received with enthusiasm from those who really mattered he had begun thinking about more music along these lines and by April, when the big split finally happened, he had already demoed a few of the songs that would later appear on their next album, the first by the new Thompson Twins, *Quick Step and Sidekick*. At the same time, John Hade had acquired a record deal for them with a major label, Arista, together with an advance of £30,000.

During that first meeting with John he was hazy about the way the band had actually split. It was clear the others were far from happy about it, but he didn't elaborate too much. Later we learned that they had simply been taken into a room at The Point – a little studio in Victoria where the band rehearsed and demoed songs – and he and Tom had sacked them.

Such things happen all the time in the pop world. It's a rough-and-tumble business where egos are smashed on a daily basis and where there is little room for gentle souls – unless they're immensely talented. The original members of the Twins were definitely talented musicians, but out of step; their approach just did not sit well with those at the helm of the band and so the partnership could not survive.

The new unit was simple, sleek and efficient. Out went guitarists John Roog and Pete Dodd, drummer Chris Bell and relatively new recruit, bassist Matthew Seligman. The Thompson Twins were now a three-piece – Tom, of course, with Alannah Currie and Joe Leeway. And now, the fourth Thompson Twin, John Hade, was bound much more closely with the other three, forming a unified, calculating and care-fully orchestrated hit-machine which, within twelve months, would shed friends and their original following but find a global audience.

John told us this story as we sat in the living room of his house in Lillieshall Road, Clapham, across the street from the tiny terraced house Tom shared with Alannah. But what did he want with us? Why were we there?

'We all loved your EP,' he said, 'and would like you to support us on the forthcoming tour.'

I could have floated through the ceiling and settled on the roof. Trying to keep cool, I glanced briefly at Jan and asked John to elaborate.

'We finish the album in a few weeks,' he began. 'Then we have six weeks of rehearsals before starting a national tour in October – colleges mainly. Then we begin the US leg which takes us to Christmas and then maybe on to Japan and Australia in the spring. We would like you to join the British leg and if that goes well, then . . .'

'But how does this work? Where's the catch?'

'There's no catch.' He looked strangely hurt. 'You'll have to provide your own transport of course, pay for accommodation, and there'll be a small standard fee, three or four grand for the whole tour.'

That was the catch. I gulped, and looking at Jan I could see the confusion in her eyes. Suddenly our euphoria drained away. We were penniless.

'Your record company will cover it all.'

'Ah, yes,' I nodded, and then thought . . . no, this is silly; be honest. But before I could say anything, Jan had intervened. 'We'll have to talk to them,' she said, uncharacteristically confident.

'Of course,' John replied. 'But in principle?'

'It sounds fantastic,' Jan exclaimed and beamed at me.

Then John made us tea, we left him with a tape of some new songs we had recorded a few weeks earlier as a two-piece synth-based unit, and thirty minutes later Jan and I were walking back to the tube, wondering what on earth we were supposed to do next.

19

Things had to be sorted out quickly. The Twins, we were told, were due back in the UK by the end of that week and they wanted to get the support organised by then. Waving goodbye to John Hade, we had said we would meet him back at his house in a few days.

That evening we called Greg and arranged to meet him in London two days later, Thursday at noon, with our meeting with John arranged for three. Those meetings, we knew, could change our lives utterly.

We had been to Greg's office before but we had never seen it looking so bleak. He was on his own in a room shrivelled to the size of a cupboard by the piles of boxes and crates stacked up around his cluttered desk. The boxes, containing vinyl destined for alternative clubs and student bedsits, spilled out into the hall in disorderly towers. Pinned to the walls but almost totally obscured were posters of some of his acts, our label-mates – Leather Nun, their charming poster boasting a particularly buxom sister brandishing a switch-blade, and further down the hall, posters for 400 Blows and the Sex Gang Children, all ultra-obscure cult bands who shifted a few thousand units across Europe. Strange bed-fellows indeed.

Greg could hardly remember what we had gone there for. He was in one of his depressed moods. I stood against the wall next to a tower of vinyl and Jan gingerly cleared a space on the desk and perched herself on a corner. Greg looked at us with expressionless eyes.

We told him the story again and he nodded in silence, then after I had filled in a few details, he sighed heavily and leaned back in his squeaky chair, rubbed his eyes and looked at each of us intently, his face softening a little. I suddenly felt really sorry for him.

'It's great they're interested,' he said slowly. 'But we can't do a thing.'

Deep inside both Jan and I knew this was coming. We had said nothing, but we knew, we knew.

'We don't have five or six grand to pay for a tour and you have nothing to promote,' he added softly.

'We could release a single,' I said automatically, but my voice betrayed my despondency.

'Not enough, Mike. Besides, Sexual Phonograph has a fucking serious cash-flow problem. We had to spend a shit-load of money on the EP,' and he raised his hands to our protests. 'It'll make a profit . . . I don't mean that, but we won't see a penny for at least three months. No, a tour, any tour, however good the opportunity for you, is just impossi-ble. I'm really sorry.'

I looked at Greg's bloodshot eyes, at the crudely produced posters, the rancid red carpet and the ripped squeaky chair he was sitting on. Between the bars over the windows years of dirt made the sky look grey and oppressive, even though the sun was shining outside. In this office it was always 4 P.M. on a cold winter's evening.

It was not Greg's fault and I'm glad to say we did not try to blame him. He had been great for us and had helped us to reach this point. It was simply that he couldn't help us take the next step. The Thompson Twins were not yet big-time by any means, but they were ICI to Greg's corner chemist.

We had time to kill and decided to walk from Fulham over the river to Clapham. Little had been said since our row a few days earlier. The atmosphere in the flat had been businesslike and clinical, and we each knew the air should be cleared but neither of us had any idea how to go about it. It was as though we had reached an unspoken agreement that we would see how this situation might play itself out and maybe try to pick up the pieces later. Knowing what Greg's reaction would be was not the only thing we had surmised; it was clear to each of us that we were now only staying together because of a potential future, a bit like those couples who keep their marriage going for the sake of the children. But at that moment it looked like the children were about to leave home prematurely and our 'marriage' was about to collapse.

The walk along Lillieshall Road with John Hade's house in sight felt like an impossibly long journey and one we didn't really want to complete, for we knew that at its end lay only embarrassment and failure. For what seemed like an age, we stood at his door, not speaking, not even looking at one another until finally Jan pushed the bell and we saw through the glass John's shape appear as he walked along the hall towards us.

He had fixed tea and we sat down again in his living room. In the background we could hear some soft jazz sax and the house was filled with the smell of jasmine from a pair of joss-sticks burning in the hall. This was no Chelsea

Mother Earth at Zero 6 in 1979. The author (left) is playing the replacement to the railway sleeper; Jan is standing far right, playing tambourine.

Bleak and industrial, after scalping.
Early 1980.

The first Rock Garden gig, 1981.

The two-piece, Colour-Me-Pop, a few days after meeting John Hade in 1982.

Watch With Mother, 1981. Jan, Martin Jago, the author and Colin McGlone.

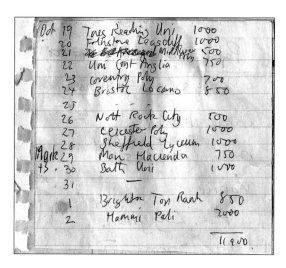

Oct 19 Toves Reading Uni, 1000
20 Folkstone Leasdiff 1000
21 ~~To be Arranged~~ Midweek 500
22 Uni Cont Anglia 750
23 Coventry Poly 700
24 Bristol Locarno 850
25
26 Nott Rock City 500
27 Leicester Poly 1000
28 Sheffield Lyceum 1000
Mark 29 Man Hacienda 750
43 . 30 Bath Uni 1000
31
1 Brighton Top Rank 850
2 Hammi Pati 2000
_____
11900

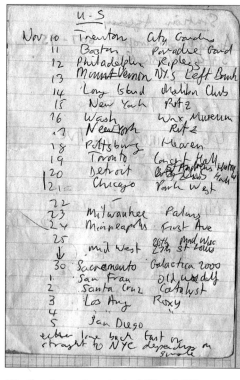

U.S

Nov 10 Trenton City Gardens
11 Boston Paradise Gard
12 Philadelphia Ripleys
13 Mount Vernon N.Y.s Left Bank
14 Long Island Malibu Club
15 New York Ritz
16 Wash Wax Museum
17 New York Ritz
18 Pittsburg Heaven
19 Toronto Concert Hall History
20 Detroit Cabbage Patch Hall
21 Chicago Park West
22
23 Milwaukee Palms
24 Minneapolis First Ave
25 mid West 26th Mad Wisc
↓ 29th St Louis
30 Sacramento Galactica 2000
1 San Fran Old woddly
2 Santa Cruz Catalyst
3 Los Ang Roxy
4
5 San Diego
either line back East or
straight to NYC depending on
Smole

*The list of tour dates in the UK and US,
scribbled down while on the phone to John Hade.*

he 'trendy tramp' look,
mmer 1982.

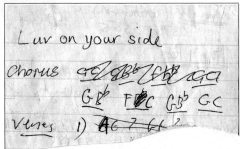

A crib sheet for the chord sequence to 'Love On
Your Side'.

Thompson Twins rehearsals at E-Z Hire,
September/October 1982: Joe (top), Jan and the
author.

TOP: *John Hade (wearing glasses) in the dressing room at the Lyceum, Sheffield.*

MIDDLE: *Sound-check in Folkestone. Tom is centre-stage, talking to a roadie; Jan at the keyboard on the left.*

BOTTOM: *The Thompson Twins at the Hammersmith Palais, 2 November 1982. Jan and the author far left; Alannah, Andrew Bodnar, Tom and Joe on the right.*

The author in Oxford, soon after leaving the Thompson Twins, thinking about a novel in the German Expressionist style.

penthouse or the New York duplex of the mega-successful manager (that sort of thing came later), but equally it was a million miles from the offices of Sexual Phonograph and it made us feel even more isolated. My stomach ached with the tension.

We decided to tell John straight away and on the walk here I had elected to be the one to break the news; how our record label could do nothing and that we could not magically produce the sort of money we needed out of thin air. He let me talk without interruption and each time I looked at his face he had a concerned expression. Once in a while he would nod or shift slightly in his chair. When I had finished, there was a painful silence for a few seconds and the jazz seemed to ebb away.

Finally, John simply said, 'Well,' and looked away towards the window and the street beyond. Then, looking back at us, he said, 'Look, Michael, Jan, it's okay. In a way I thought this was going to happen.'

We must have looked stunned because he immediately went on. 'No offence, but I know your label is small and that the money might be a sticking point. So, I have another idea. I've been talking to the band about you, and I FedExed your tape to them, I hope you don't mind . . . They love it.'

Startled, I made to reply but he held up a hand. 'As I explained the other day, we're now a three-piece, but we need a band for the tour. What would you say to joining the Thompson Twins as keyboard players?'

I remember the moment as though it were this morning. I remember the instant sense of relief, of hope, the pain in my stomach vanishing. It was not one of those more usual revelations, the type that takes time to sink in, this was instant. I could hardly bring myself to look at Jan, but when I did she had turned to me at the same moment and was beaming; it was the only time I had seen her smile since we were last here.

'Good idea?' John said with a grin.

I was lost for words, but Jan was already in there. 'No,' she said, 'it's a fantastic idea.'

'We'll have to sort out quite a few things, of course,' John added. 'So will you . . .'

'Of course,' Jan and I said in unison.

'But I think we could work well together.'

'Absolutely,' Jan said without hesitation. I just nodded, but then a thought struck me. 'What about our own careers?' I asked and I instantly sensed Jan stiffen beside me. I knew that if I looked at her now her stare would be none too friendly.

'I've been thinking about that too,' John replied without missing a beat, and I felt Jan relax again. 'Of course, it's entirely up to you two, but I thought, okay, you may have to put your careers on hold for a few months but our management and publishing company could handle things for you independently of the Twins and maybe next year we could go for a deal with Colour-Me-Pop.'

This was almost too much and it didn't sink in immediately. It just seemed natural to nod and say knowingly: 'Yes, of course, that sounds brilliant!' Which it did.

And so there we sat, transformed. Five minutes had taken us from despair to euphoria, from trashed dreams to glittering hope. At last, at long, long last, it seemed as though all the hard work, the determination and the sheer desperate ambition were bringing their returns. Today had brought long-awaited pay dirt, big-time.

20

When we got back to the flat we really didn't know what to do with ourselves. It had been a phenomenal week. We had almost broken up, I had graduated (Jan received her results a week later), we had learned our record had a limited life-span, we had been invited on a Thompson Twins tour as support, then lost it and were then asked to join the band.

We had left Clapham in jubilant spirits and we were still on a high. Shaking hands with John at the door to his house, he had promised to sort out the details and to contact us soon with the arrangements to meet Tom, Alannah and Joe. For our part, we had some organising to do too. But we decided on the train back that we would say nothing to anyone until John called with the details, even though we could hardly contain our excitement. Luckily he rang a couple of hours later.

'Okay,' he said straight away, 'you got a pen?' I found a scrap of paper and began scribbling.

'The Twins are finishing off the album at Rak Studios in St John's Wood. Do you know it?'

'I know of it,' I replied.

'They'll be there for a few weeks. It would be great if you could come along and meet the band so we can all get to know one another a little better. Would next Tuesday be any good?'

I wanted to say I'd have to consult my busy schedule, but just said: 'Yes, of course.'

'About two?'

'That's fine.'

'Right, rehearsals begin in four weeks at E-Z Hire in Islington. Do you know it?'

'I know of it,' I replied.

And this time John gave a quick laugh. 'Sorry.'

'That's okay.'

'We rehearse for six weeks. You and Jan can pick up the rough mixes of the album when we meet at Rak and Tom will give you the music. You've got a decent keyboard?'

'It's all right – a string synth.'

'Hum, that's no good, I'll arrange for a Prophet V to be delivered, it'll save time later.'

I must have looked completely stunned (and I was) because Jan gave me a funny look. I just mouthed 'PRO-PH-ET V' and she rolled her eyes and mouthed back 'F-U-C-K!' It was the very best synth money could buy.

'Is that okay?'

'Yes, yes, of course it is . . . Great.'

'Right, I've made a note of it. It'll take a day or two.'

'Oh, that's fine,' I answered, trying to keep my voice calm, but by now I was alternately leaping up and down silently on the spot and throwing back my head, my eyes tightly shut.

'I guess you'll have to arrange a place to live for the six weeks before we hit the road. I might have a few contacts. I'll make a note of it, get a few people to contact you.'

'Thanks.'

'Right then, the tour dates. First gig is Reading University on October 19th. We then do twelve dates, with 25th and 30th October off. The final date is the Hammersmith Palais on November 2nd.'

I could hardly believe it. I had only been at the Hammersmith Palais a couple of days earlier, in the audience at the Gang of Four gig. In about two months from now, I thought, I'll be on the same stage. It felt utterly surreal.

Suddenly, I realised John was talking again. 'Michael, are you there?'

'Yeah, yeah, sorry. I'm just scribbling this down.' But actually I was beginning to experience a sort of sensory overload.

'Okay, next, the US leg of the tour. First date, Trenton on November 10th.'

'Trenton? Where's that?'

'Just outside New York.'

'Fuck!'

John laughed again. 'Then it's Boston on the 11th, Phili 12th, back to New York, then Washington. Basically all the major cities throughout November and December.' And he gave the details. '. . . finishing off with a date at the Roxy in LA on December 3rd with perhaps a Christmas gig in New York. After that . . .' And by now John was speeding off so fast that I could hardly keep up. 'We'll soon have dates for the spring in Japan, Australia and more in the US. What do you think?'

Naturally, I didn't know what to say. I was just gaping at Jan as she tried to get the gist of what we were saying and periodically peering over my shoulder amazed at what I was writing on the scrap of paper, the details of what we thought would be our future lives spilling out upon the page.

'Oh yes, money.'

And for a second I thought . . . What? And we get paid too?

'You'll get all expenses, a daily allowance and £150 each per week during the tour, but basically that all goes in your bank . . . you won't need to spend a penny on the road. And then there're your own projects, which we'll talk about when we've got a bit more settled, agreed?'

'Well, what can I say?' I replied, grinning like a teenage lemming on a mud slide.

'Any questions, just call me, okay?'

'Absolutely, and we'll get things sorted out our end,' I said with as much professionalism as I could muster. 'We look forward to next Tuesday. And John . . . thanks.'

'Don't mention it.'

The phone went down, our old lives were consigned to history, and the next stage of our journey had begun.

21

So what were we supposed to do now? We began by staggering our friends and families with our news, then we gave
notice on the flat, cancelled the milk, had the post re-routed,
picked up a dozen cardboard boxes from the local supermarket and used them to pack our few possessions, sent back the
rented TV and video; with the dregs of our final grant
cheques we paid the outstanding phone, gas and electricity
bills and when the Prophet V arrived we could not be
dragged away from it as we started to learn the Thompson
Twins' songs for the tour. And when all this was done, we
invited our close friends to a house-freezing party.

In the middle of all this, my old friend and our first
bassist, Tim Alexander, was about to embark on his own
great adventure. His band, Fragment, had decided to move
to Holland to see what fortune might offer them. He and
some of the band were living in a rundown flat a short walk

away, and taking a break from our own preparations, I popped round to see how his were coming along.

If there had been a prize for most organised band in the world, Fragment would have won it. When I arrived, their newly acquired ten-year-old Transit van was on the drive and they were building a sleeping area in the back behind the cabin. On each side of the van lay piles of equipment and boxes filled with cables, guitars and bits of drums. The idea was that the three of them plus a roadie/engineer would travel in the van to Holland, sleep in the back and break into the rock scene by busking in the streets of Rotterdam and playing at any venue that would have them. When they could, they would rent a communal apartment and see how things panned out.

Amazingly, things panned out and they did exactly what they set out to do. The three original members are still together, all married with children, mortgages and recording studios, playing two hundred dates a year and recording the odd album when they feel like it.

I managed to drag Tim away and we went for a walk along the cliffs overlooking the sea. It was hot and we shared a large bottle of Coke. We were both excited about what we were doing, but there was an underlying sadness about it all. Both of us knew we were stepping out into the void, making another move away from convention, from normality. And both of us felt, but had never articulated, the fear that we might be making a big mistake. But then, both of us were aware we really had little to lose.

'You okay about what's happening?' Tim asked after we had sat down on a bench. We were both staring at the sea.

'I could ask you exactly the same question,' I replied. 'And we'd probably give the same answers.'

He laughed. 'Crazy really. Who would have thought it?'

'It's what I've been struggling for all these years.'

'Yeah, I know. And Jan?'

I looked at him, then away towards the waves. I hadn't told him, but he knew we were shaky. 'I hope it's what she wants, but I'm not at all sure.'

'Perhaps she doesn't appreciate you anymore, Mike.'

I shrugged.

'After all,' he went on. 'What else could she expect from life? She's a good singer, but what's she likely to do otherwise, teach? Big fucking deal.'

I nodded but said nothing for a while and took a swig of the Coke. 'Hey, come on,' I exclaimed, handing him the bottle. 'We're supposed to be at a turning point in our lives. We're young, free and maybe nearly single. Let's enjoy it, yeah?'

I jumped up and ran across the grass, down the incline towards steps that descended to a bridge that crossed the railway line and led on to the beach beyond. I could feel the hot breeze against my face and taste the salty air. Soon, I would be in London, in a rehearsal studio, I thought. Then I'd be playing before audiences across the planet. I had visions of yellow cab-rides the length of Fifth Avenue and running barefoot along the sand of Venice Beach.

A moment later Tim was beside me.

'You coming tonight?' I asked, referring to our house-freezing party.

''Course,' he said matter-of-factly, handing me the last of the drink.

The flat looked good even with the walls bare of pictures and the shelves emptied of books. That night was the antithesis of the 1967 theme party of three years earlier; only the people we really cared about had been invited and the mood was a strange blend of regret, hope and excitement.

One of the people I had asked along, an art student called Helen Howard whom I had met a year or two earlier, brought along the local paper, the *Evening Echo*. It carried a story about Jan and me. Under the banner 'COLOUR-ME DUO BECOME TWINS', we read:

Things are really happening for Mike and Jan, the nucleus of Southend's exciting musical team Colour-Me-Pop. They have just joined the Thompson Twins, the cult British band as keyboard players. Next month they embark on a tour of Britain with the band and on November 5th they fly on to New York. Mike and Jan are understandably excited about the events of the last few weeks which look set to change their lives completely. Jan said: 'The record company is paying for us to have new hair-dos and lots of bright clothes so that when we walk into the New York clubs people know we are with the Thompson Twins.'

'I didn't say that!' Jan exclaimed loudly to the room, reading the piece over my shoulder.

'Oh, you poor love . . . misquoted already!' Helen quipped and Jan laughed.

'Better get used to it,' I added. And we all raised our glasses to the *Evening Echo*.

Much later, with the drink drunk and the dope smoked, at the door to the flat we said goodbye to each of our friends, hugged and laughed, kissed and cried a little. To each we gave one of the house plants that had dotted our bookcases and the windowsills and each of our friends wished us good fortune.

Tim was the last to leave and I stood with him at the gate to the street. We shook hands and embraced. 'Well, good luck, mate,' I said quietly.

'And you too,' he replied. 'And you too.'

22

We first met the Thompson Twins at Rak Studios in St John's Wood. They were finishing some of the vocal and percussion tracks for the album *Quick Step and Sidekick*, which was to become their first international hit album and spawn a series of Top 20 singles.

But at the time the Thompson Twins were relatively unknown. They had a devoted collection of a few thousand fans who had followed them around the country to concerts in obscure places in tiny halls and clubs and who faithfully bought their earliest records. But now the band were on the verge of bigger things. And this is not a judgement made with the benefit of hindsight – there was an indefinable air of confidence surrounding the entity that was the Thompson Twins, a feeling that pervaded the band, the management, the record company, the publicists and publishers, something you could sense as soon as you entered their world.

If it wasn't for the fact that Jan and I had been invited to join the band, we would have found Rak Studios immensely intimidating. We had been to some studios in our time, but nowhere like this. We arrived in our twelve-year-old puke-green Vauxhall Viva with a dodgy clutch (£125 from the *Evening Echo* auto ads six months earlier), both feeling exhausted and hungover from the party. A sweep of white steps led to the flat-fronted Georgian terrace in NW1; it looked more like the offices of a successful PR firm than a recording studio. There would be no rotting sofas or piss-stained carpets here, I thought, as I pushed open the huge glass door at the entrance and strode, with fabricated chutz-pah, to the hardwood reception desk about three miles away along the corridor.

'Michael and Jan,' I said to the girl behind the desk, an ultra-cool-looking babe. She had bandages plaited into her hair, huge black-lined eyes and wore what looked like four different old men's vests that between them just managed to create something vaguely opaque. It was a look six months ahead of its time and later seen by the world in at least two Madonna videos. 'We've come to see John Hade and the Thompson Twins,' I added as she looked at me blankly. In the background I could hear a tape of that horrible song by a group of little black kids called Musical Youth, something about 'passing the dutchie from the left-hand side . . .'

'Oh yeah,' she replied with sudden warmth. 'You're Colour-Me-Pop, the new members of the band, right?'

I was stunned.

'I've just been reading about you,' she went on. 'Look.' And she turned round the copy of *NME* she had been read-ing and there was a headline, 'PLUTONIUM BLONDES', and a lengthy piece about the EP. We had missed the paper that week and could hardly believe what she was showing us. 'And,' she said with great emphasis, 'here's the indie chart, you're Number 22 this week.' Then she leaned towards us conspiratorially and whispered, 'That's higher than the last Thompson Twins single got to!'

Regaining some equilibrium, I laughed politely and thought, I love this woman, I want to grow old with her. I almost said it, but while I stood gawping at the receptionist's four vests, Jan had found out from her where we should go and turned me towards a door further down the corridor.

We could hear voices and laughter from the other side of the door. We knocked, but it was ignored, so Jan peeked in and then we stepped into the room together.

I didn't recognise anyone at first, but I knew none of the Thompson Twins were there. A group of three men were playing darts. 'Hello there,' one of them said as he turned and continued to throw his dart without looking at the board.

We introduced ourselves, and a wiry, bald black guy stood up from a table and stepped forward, his hand extended, a big smile spread across his face. 'Hi, my name's Errol Brown,' he said. 'We're Hot Chocolate. What're you guys doing here?'

'We're with the Thompson Twins,' I blurted out, and instantly felt weird. It was the first time I had actually said that.

'Cool,' he said in the coolest way imaginable. 'You wanna play some darts?'

And so it was that when five minutes later Tom Bailey walked into the room followed closely by John Hade, Alannah Currie and Joe Leeway, Jan and I were being so soundly thrashed at darts by Hot Chocolate we hardly noticed them.

By this stage in our careers I had experienced some inspiring and depressing moments and had seen a few things, but meeting Tom for the first time was something special. I think it was not merely that I was meeting a musician whom I admired immensely, whose records I had bought and to whose status I aspired, but I knew that we were going to be

working together from now on, that we were even going to be
in the same band. In the space of a few weeks I had taken
that enormous and incredibly rare journey from fan to fellow
band member.

We all shook hands and smiled at one another. We com-
plimented them on their tans and the backing tracks we had
been sent and Tom was especially ebullient about the songs
of ours he had heard. Alannah gave the immediate impres-
sion of being shy but covered her insecurities with
brashness. I can honestly say I didn't like her from the first
moment we met. And perhaps because of this I could never
pierce her protective shield, and never got to know the true
Alannah. Now, sadly, I only have memories of a rather
spoilt, self-protective woman who seemed to possess a deep
well of bitterness towards many of those around her. With
hindsight I can see that the seeds of my unhappiness with
the Thompson Twins were planted in part that first day we
met.

In complete contrast, I found Tom to be one of the
warmest, most intelligent and attractive people I have ever
met. As much as I knew I would never truly relate to
Alannah, I at once felt drawn towards Tom and knew he and
I would really hit it off. Joe, I also liked immediately. He
seemed a lot older than his years. He never pretended to be a
great musician but was a skilled actor who had performed
Shakespeare at the Young Vic and could have been treading
the boards rather than dancing upon them if he had wished.

We all went off together and sat in a room nearby. Cups of
tea appeared from nowhere. 'So, you like the idea of joining
the band,' Tom said.

'Of course,' Jan and I said together.

Then Alannah leaned forward. 'You see, we have this idea
to pair everyone up as twins.'

'There are two other new members, Andy and Boris,
they'll be here later,' Tom added. 'Andrew Bodnar's a great

bassist and Boris Williams is the coolest drummer, but neither of them can be "twinned up",' he added.

'But we thought that you, Jan, could be made to look more like Alannah,' Joe said. 'And Michael . . . well, you and Tom look pretty alike.' Tom and I looked at one another, and as if for the first time, I saw the resemblance. I had mousy hair at the time and Tom had already adopted his trademark red spiky haircut, but apart from that we really could have been brothers. He is a few years older than me, but we were the same height and build, and our facial features were close. Alannah and Jan would present more of a problem, I thought, but I could see what they were getting at.

To be honest, we probably would have agreed to shave off our eyebrows and wear mouse costumes if that had been required of us. But we also thought the idea of twinning us was a good one.

'It should be a laugh anyway,' Alannah said, waving her hand in the air nonchalantly. 'And you're happy about putting your own careers on ice for a while?'

I looked at Jan and we both nodded. 'I think Jan would agree,' I said, 'that we'll gain experience from touring and be stronger for it when we re-group.'

'You're doing really well though,' Tom added.

'Yeah, but I think we need to write some new material for an album next year maybe,' I turned to Jan and she was nodding. 'I'm sure we could find time to do some of our own stuff between gigs.'

'I wouldn't bet on it,' Alannah chipped in.

But Tom just gave me a knowing look. 'Come on,' he said, getting up from the table. 'Let's show you the studio, we've just finished the next single.'

To me, the inside of Studio 1 at Rak looked like a set from *2001: A Space Odyssey*. The main recording room was at least forty foot by thirty and housed a grand piano, an array of the most incredible synthesisers, an ensemble of

percussion instruments, congas, bongos, a rack of tambourines and various shaky things. At one end was an
electronic drum kit with a huge gong behind it, and scattered
around the room were a veritable forest of microphone
stands. Huge convex plastic discs had been suspended from
the ceiling some twenty feet above our heads and the walls
were covered with vast mahogany rectangles – both were to
improve the acoustics.

We wandered around the room, Joe played chopsticks on
the piano and Jan and I tried hard not to look like complete
novices.

'This is where it all happens,' Tom said and led us to the
rack of keyboards. 'On stage, we'll use the Prophet V and the
Oberheim, they give the full range of textures we want.
Anyway, let's go into the mixing room and play you what
we've done.'

Tom again led the way out of the recording room and
along the corridor, through another heavy, tightly sealed door
into the mixing room.

And it was vast. The biggest studio Jan and I had been
into was an eight-track. All our material, including the EP,
had either been recorded in one of the many ropy back-room
studios we had paid one hundred and fifty to two hundred
pounds a day for, or else on a borrowed four-track at the flat
or in friends' bedrooms. Of course, this place was in an
entirely different league. It was a state-of-the-art twenty-
four-track studio which had the very latest in studio
technology – at least a million pounds' worth of equipment
sat in that room alone.

Today, recording methods are very different. Most bands
who reach the level of the Thompson Twins record in a digital forty-eight-track studio. Everything is now recorded on
to computers, digitally manipulated and synthesised, and in
some unnameable cases the vocals are also 'manufactured'.
But in 1982, everything was played manually (with the

exception of the occasional use of a machine called a sequencer, which still had to be programmed manually). The recording was analogue, the music went straight on to tape, just as we had done many times since our first attempts at Crazy Sound. In twenty-four-track studios they just employed bigger, better tape. The Twins used a drum machine, but it was nothing like the Duracell bunny we still relied upon, but a thing called a Linn drum which was many years ahead of its time and produced a crackingly realistic imitation of a drummer.

I stared in silence at the racks of equipment and dreamed of the day I could come into a place like this with my own songs and spend months over an album, just as Tom was now doing. But, for the moment at least, this would do just fine.

Tom introduced us to their producer, a tall, chunky, handsome American named Alex Sadkin. He stood up and shook hands, enveloping Jan's tiny fingers with his huge paw. He sat at a massive mixing console that ran the length of the room, before him a sea of buttons and sliders, each of which performed a very specific task. I could hardly imagine how he kept track of everything.

But then, Alex Sadkin was one of the great producers of the early 1980s, and by the time we met he had already worked with some of the best and most famous names in the pop world. This, I knew, was another sign the Twins were on a steep ascendant; people like Alex Sadkin only worked with the best, and he did not come cheap. A fitness fanatic who referred to a coffee buzz as 'floating tension' and never touched alcohol, tea or coffee throughout the time I knew him, he was mourned as a great character and a unique producer when he died a couple of years later in a car crash in the Caribbean.

Tom sat in the only other chair in the room next to Alex and they rewound the tape, each of them manipulating a few

controls. Then, suddenly, the room was awash with the opening percussion and drum track of 'Lies'.

It was very loud, but it would have sounded amazing on a
tinny radio (which of course was exactly the desired effect).
Jan and I had heard the backing tracks (the drums and bass)
on tapes we had used to rehearse with in the flat, but hearing
the finished product over these speakers in this setting was
just incredible.

To be honest, the new Thompson Twins did not have a
unique sound. The Human League had already had a string
of hits from *Dare*, Depeche Mode were a powerful pop entity
and The Eurythmics were bubbling under, but the Twins
had found a niche within this genre, and aside from the synthetic nature of their new songs, they did not actually sound
precisely like anyone else around at the time. Today, we may
think the sound of the '80s has a certain sameness, but if
you really listen and think about it, it is only the shared technology and the obsession we all had with danceable rhythms
(the *de rigueur* 120 beats per minute) that creates this effect.

I stood against the back wall with the others. In front of
me sat one of the most famous producers in the world and
next to him Tom Bailey, his spiky red mop moving in time to
the incessant beat. Beyond the desk, through the glass stood
the recording room in all its vastness, recessed spots picking
out the chrome of the percussion and the deep ebony body of
the magnificent Steinway.

And I was to be part of this, I thought, allowing the idea to
really seep into my consciousness for the first time. Finally, I
had arrived.

23

The Thompson Twins were a great team. Tom was the musician, and although all their songs were credited equally to the three of them, he played everything and sang 99 per cent of the vocals with the odd gimmicky 'rap' or backing warble left to Joe and Alannah. Tom had been classically trained and had taught music for a short time. He was also totally in tune with the musical zeitgeist of 1982. But although Alannah and Joe didn't know as much about music, they possessed other important qualities.

I had learned long before joining the Thompson Twins that pop stardom was about 1 per cent to do with musical ability. Indeed, some have argued that being able to play is actually a hindrance. Pop has always been 99 per cent image, and the vast majority of aspiring pop musicians fail not because they make the wrong music but because they have the wrong ideas about their image. So, in their own ways,

Alannah and Joe were every bit as important as Tom to the success of the new Thompson Twins. Alannah was the self-appointed stylist for the band. She had an eye for fashion just as Tom had an ear for pop, and she laid down strict rules about how the band should dress, how we should behave and the way the videos and album sleeves should look.

Everyone involved in the Twins now realised that to succeed the group had to present a complete package, a corporate image. It was all about marketing. Tom could bury himself in the studio, but it was up to Alannah (with John Hade's encouragement) to organise The Package.

For me, though, Alannah went too far. She created a written manifesto which outlined the aims and targets of the band. This was fine, but it spilled over into all aspects of our lives. None of us was allowed to take photographs of any of the others in the band at any time. The reason for this was a paranoia concerning the pirating of images and the chance that a photograph of one of us looking 'inappropriate' might be leaked to the press when the tour began and the records started charting. We all had to wear super-trendy clothes anywhere outside of our homes, even in rehearsals, and when we socialised as a group we had to present a unified image and to carry ourselves in a particular way. I remember her once telling me I smiled too much. 'David Bowie never smiles,' she added frostily before walking off. That certainly wiped the smile from my face.

Joe added a third and vital element to the brew. As a trained actor he knew how to present the band on stage and it was largely thanks to him that we had such striking stage sets. For the *Quick Step and Sidekick* tour Joe devised a sort of post-industrial *Wizard of Oz* image using screens to project cartoon-like machines spewing steam and workmen wielding giant mallets. Joe also understood the dynamics of performance, whether it was Ibsen or a forty-minute pop concert, and he knew how the songs should interact with the images.

It was a great team and it became immensely successful, but they needed musicians to create a real band for performances and to breathe life into songs that worked extremely well on vinyl but had to be translated into powerful set pieces live.

Jan and I went to Rak every day for the two weeks leading up to the start of rehearsals. We didn't have much to do but to hang out and talk to the other musicians who frequented the place at the same time. We got to know Nick Heyward, who had recently split from Haircut 100 and was recording some solo material. Hot Chocolate were there for most of the two weeks and we never once beat them at darts. We saw the studio owner, Mickie Most, come and go, really just a fleeting glimpse of peroxide streaks, wrinkles and a shiny Rolls-Royce; but then we would have been disappointed if he had arrived at Rak on a moped.

It was a heady time, when fashion and music were going through something of a transformation, again. The days of the New Romantics were gone and the bands who had epitomised that scene were gradually changing. Spandau Ballet were one of the biggest bands of the time and no strangers to updating their image. They had struggled and clawed their way to success and in the early days had done everything they could to gain publicity. I remember sitting in the bar of the ICA in the Mall sometime in 1980, just before some no-hope band called Pink Military were due to appear, when I was astonished to see entering the bar five guys in the worst drag costumes ever. They looked like the old women in Monty Python, all hairy legs and misshapen over-sized boobs. But although I was surprised to see them, it was clear this was not the first such prank they had pulled. I overheard someone nearby say in weary notes, 'Oh God, it's Spandau Ballet again!'

The Spands (as the DJs loved to call them) and Duran

Duran were still up there selling the most and peering down from a million teenagers' bedroom walls, but others were beginning to edge them aside. Grown-ups didn't take much notice of Duran Duran, Adam Ant or Spandau Ballet, and other musicians who had once been considered underground or alternative were emerging into the spotlight with some interesting music. The Human League had also split into two, creating Heaven 17 and a new version of the Human League which became the mega-successful entity fronted by Phil Oakey and the two schoolgirls, Joanne Catherall and Susanne Sulley, he found in a disco dancing round their handbags. The Eurythmics had emerged from a rock group called The Tourists and were on the verge of having their first hit, and of course Yazoo had spun off from Depeche Mode. Summer 1982 was the time of Culture Club's first single, 'Do You Really Want To Hurt Me?' and New Order were preparing to enter the scene by beginning the recording sessions that led to 'Blue Monday', one of the biggest-selling singles of all time and perhaps the single of the decade.

It was a long, bright summer, warm into September. It was the summer of the Falklands War and Poland was under martial law. Italy won the World Cup, Grace Kelly was killed in a car crash and Diana gave birth to Prince William. The look of summer '82 was dubbed 'trendy tramp' or 'tatty chic'. We wore angle-length jeans and Chinese slippers (£1.50 from Camden market), clothes worn in multiple layers, coloured string vests over T-shirts, lengths of bandage and strips of leather wrapped around our wrists, and we all had Big Hair.

The year before, both Jan and I had flirted with the 1930s look. I had bought old suits for £1 from Oxfam and coupled them with buttoned-down shirts, spotted ties and braces and Jan wore tight skirts and tops or flowing dresses. I grew my hair and greased it back to create a Clark Gable look and Jan curled her hair to make her look like Greta Garbo or Bette

Davis. Now everything had changed. When we met, Tom
had spiky red hair, adapted from the long post-hippie locks
he had affected in the original band. He had had the sides
shaved, leaving a long pony tail which he plaited in a style
later dubbed the 'prat plait'. Alannah had shaved her head in
high sweeps over each ear and left the rest as a bush and Joe
had dreadlocks that appeared to spring from nowhere in
clumps all over his head. So, one of the first things Alannah
did with Jan and me was to arrange for new hairstyles.

It took all day to transform my 1930s cut to a 'Thompson
Twin special', and when it was done and I emerged from
Strands hairdressers just off Oxford Street I felt utterly
ridiculous. Heading for Regent Street and the underground
station at Piccadilly Circus I thought the entire world was
looking at me and giggling. And they probably were – but
then, wasn't that the idea? Besides, all I needed to do to
dampen my self-consciousness was to recall the warm glow as
I told the stylist to put my £150 bill on the Thompson
Twins' account.

I soon got used to the haircut, shaved sides, spiky on top
and dyed black around the ears and bright orange above that.
In fact I grew so attached to it I kept it in a similar style for
at least a year after leaving the band. And now Tom and I
really did look like twins. In breaks during the recording of
finishing touches to the album, he and I would sometimes go
into town together. Whenever we were asked, with a nod we
would silently confirm the idea we were real twins.

And as my friendship with Tom grew, I began to dislike
Alannah more and more, and I knew the feeling was mutual.
We never had an argument, we just avoided each other. I
suppose in some ways she may have seen Jan and me as
something of a threat. We were both musicians with some
limited success, whereas her ideas were as yet untested.
Maybe, for this reason, she didn't like me becoming too
friendly with Tom, because she seemed able to cope with

Jan better than she could with me. I think this fear was just an expression of insecurity; Tom and Alannah were a strong partnership and she had nothing to fear. They were lovers and business partners, and although during my time with the band they were going through a frail period in their personal relationship, any worries she had about me forming a musical unit with Tom were, as time proved, quite misplaced.

On the other hand there is the distinct possibility she thought I was an idiot; and in some ways I can now see why. Once, a week or so after we had met and Jan and I had become accustomed to our lives in the studio, I walked in on Alannah just as she was completing a percussion part for 'Love On Your Side', the song that became their first big hit.

I still don't understand how I could have been so dumb. The red light was on over the door to the recording room, and it wasn't a small red light, in fact it was huge. But there it is. She completely lost her cool and only just managed to stop herself from throwing her drumsticks at me. I was mortified, but my apologies met deaf ears and it took days for her to bring herself to talk to me again.

Afterwards, I thought long and hard about that incident and even now I feel a tremor of shame when I think of my own stupidity, but then again, I do think she over-reacted a little. After all, musicians expect to go through many takes to get things right in the studio. It was only years later that someone pointed out the obvious, that perhaps Alannah had been on 'take 97' when I barged in.

During the first week at Rak, Jan and I met the other two new Thompson Twins, Andrew Bodnar and Boris Williams. Andrew was very tall and very thin. He was a few years older than us and an immensely accomplished musician. He had played with Elvis Costello and had received royalty cheques for playing bass on 'I Love The Sound Of Breaking Glass',

Nick Lowe's biggest hit, from 1978. He had been everywhere, done everything, and in a way, I felt more in awe of
Andrew than I did any of the original Twins. He seemed
much older than his age, although he didn't look it and had
been in rehab for an alcohol problem when Jan and I were
freshers. He was, I quickly decided, someone from whom I
could learn a great deal, and I did.

Boris knew Andrew well. He too was a little older than us
but he was one of the most respected session musicians in the
country and had played on several hit singles as well as touring with professional bands for years. Both Andrew and
Boris made me feel like a kid, a charlatan even, and I only
managed to ward off my own insecurity by remembering
that Jan and I were very different musicians from Boris and
Andrew. I was principally a songwriter, while they were
guns-for-hire. I knew that when the time was right I would
go on to produce my own records again, and they would
move on to the next tour with the next band. Neither
approach was better than the other – they were just different.

And so, two weeks after Jan and I had said goodbye to our
friends and taken the plunge by moving into a tiny room in a
house in Highgate owned by a friend of John Hade's, *Quick
Step and Sidekick* was finished and rehearsals for the first
tour of the new band were about to begin. Every stage of our
careers up to this point had been marked by a shift in direction, a new set of instruments and sounds, new songs, and of
course, new hairstyles. Now we would have to show our true
mettle. I believed in Jan, but I wasn't at all sure I could live
up to the expectations that had been placed upon me since
our first meeting with John Hade. But I would certainly give
it my best shot.

24

For me, rehearsals had always been sporadic, sometimes rather vague affairs. But rehearsals gel a band – without them, scrappy as they often are, there is little point in a group existing at all. We rehearsed with the specific intention of readying ourselves for gigs occasionally lined up for weeks ahead, but they were also the centre of our social lives.

They usually took up the whole of each Saturday and one evening a week and they were the times we met up with our closest friends (the other members of the band), messed around, drank cheap lager and tried to forge a revolutionary, epoch-changing sound. More often than not, everyone I associated with in music put 100 per cent effort into the first three of these activities and I found myself, year in year out, trying to coax those with me into spending at least a little time on the fourth. Needless to say, rehearsals with the Thompson Twins were quite different.

John Hade had booked a rehearsal room in a dedicated complex called E-Z Hire in Islington. This was a series of warehouse-sized rooms in which bands encamped to prepare for a tour. We had a mid-sized room at the end of a driveway, third in a line of rehearsal spaces. The main room was heavily sound-proofed and it had a concrete floor covered with cheap, worn carpet. It was cold and stark, a shell about forty foot square packed with equipment. Basic strip lights hung from the low ceiling casting everywhere a pale greenish glow that made us all look jaundiced, but the place served its purpose admirably and for the next six weeks it was our home.

When I joined the Thompson Twins the biggest change for me was not what most people would have expected. I was not suddenly rich, I was not instantly recognised when I walked down the street, I did not become a heroin addict, and sadly, I did not get to sleep with coach-loads of young women. The biggest and most rewarding change was that suddenly I had everything done for me.

For years I had driven the van, carried the gear, set up the equipment, been sound engineer, set designer, roadie, not to mention songwriter, manager and musician, now all I had to do was turn up, play keyboards and have fun. It was a weird, disorientating experience but also quite wonderful. It felt like I had left the office job and jumped a cruise to the Caribbean.

On the first day, Jan and I caught the tube to King's Cross because over the weekend, the Vauxhall Viva had had a near-death experience after suffering clutch failure that called for emergency surgery. But, because the only things we had to take with us were a book and a Walkman, it represented no real problem. We arrived at the heavy doors to the rehearsal room and pressed the buzzer. Tom came to the door, mug of coffee in hand. He looked the happiest I had seen him, relaxed and evidently excited.

The room had been prepared with care and precision. To

one side stood a pair of synths on stands. Jan and I had a keyboard each but would swap occasionally. Hanging from the stands were tambourines and other assorted instruments for the ubiquitous percussion arrangements that still punctuated the Thompson Twins' songs. Over each keyboard stood a microphone because we were expected to help with backing vocals, a thought that obviously pleased Jan. Alongside the keyboards was an amp for Andrew, the bassist, and his two bass guitars were already perched on stands and tuned. Next came the drums. This was a state-of-the-art electronic kit. Unlike a conventional kit with a row of cylindrical drums of different sizes, this consisted of thin black plastic hexagons each of which was wired up to a powerful sound system. When you hit the drum it felt rock hard, but produced a really punchy sound through huge speakers either side of the room. Behind the drum stool was the obligatory rack of percussion for Boris to scratch, scrape or rattle as he deemed fit. On the opposite side of the room to the keyboards were two more sets of percussion, some congas for Joe and some timpani for Alannah. Facing into the vague circle made by these instruments stood Tom's mic and stand. Dotted around the room were large speakers through which all the instruments were fed from a mixing desk and we each had monitors at our feet through which we could have individualised mixes from the p.a. Close to the door was a mixing console where two sound men sat all day adjusting levels and practising their roles for the tour.

The final element was the tape system. During the recording of *Quick Step and Sidekick*, the Twins had decided they would use tapes to enhance the live sound. This would have been anathema to the original band, but then Tom and Alannah seemed to want to deliberately break the old rules and methods. With the sort of high-production sound the band now created in the studio, they knew they could take one of two alternative routes for the tour. They could go for a rougher, more 'authentic' sound which would not truly represent the album (and for this they would have needed a twelve-piece band rather than a seven-piece), or we could use tapes containing some of the rhythm tracks and sequencers which would fill out the sound.

They chose the second route. This meant that each song began with a 'click track', a tap, tap, tap, tap from the tape and we would all launch in. For this to work, Boris had to have a special monitoring system, requiring him to wear headphones so he could keep time with the click. At appropriate moments a bit of music would come in on the tape to supplement what we were doing. It was at once stifling and uplifting, but actually Jan and I were quite used to the idea because we had done something similar a couple of years earlier when we played live as a three-piece. It was a method used by many bands at the time, and although some people thought it was a form of fakery, this criticism was unfair. The Twins merely used tapes to add colour here and there, but there were some who took the concept much too far and did whole shows where they mimed throughout and some who even pretended they were playing for real. In this way, the truly awful two-piece Milli Vanilli was flushed down the toilet of the pop world.

The first day of rehearsals was frightening, and a little disheartening. We all knew the songs, especially Tom, Joe and Alannah, but it always takes a while for a band to gel. Fortunately, everyone there was experienced enough to know this, and no one was expecting us to instantly burst into perfect song as though we were on the set of *Oliver!*.

When the sound levels had been adjusted and everyone was comfortable, Tom suggested we have a go at 'Lies' and just see how it went. The click track came in and we were off.

I remember feeling so nervous I thought my fingers would fail me and stiffen up so I could not play the keyboard. Before that day I had only played in my band with Jan and people I had known for a long time, none of whom were really any more accomplished or successful than me. Most importantly, I had always played my songs and for a lot of the time I had played only guitar, with which I felt confident. Here I was: employed, paid, rehearsing with people whom I had seen on TV only a few months earlier, whose records I had bought. For the first time in my life, I was playing alongside real, professional musicians like Andrew and Boris. What if I fucked up?

But I didn't. The first run through of 'Lies' produced a version almost unrecognisable to any of us, and when the last note faded away there was a dreadful silence before the whole lot of us burst out laughing (even though rock stars were not meant to smile). But the ice was broken. The second attempt was infinitely better, and after our first morning, we knew things were going to work out; on a musical level at least.

25

Our new temporary home in Highgate was a single room in a slightly tatty but pleasingly Bohemian house owned by a fashion designer who specialised in heavily patterned dresses and jackets for women. We were hardly there except to sleep, and even then we usually got home long after the others living there had gone to bed and left after they had gone to work, so we hardly saw the designer or her family. Our car, we learned, would take two weeks to repair, so we caught the tube each day and grew to be glad of it; it gave us time to talk and to think.

Our relationship had improved a little, probably because we were so busy and so excited by what had happened. But there remained a certain frostiness between us, and if I had been pinned to a wall with a gun to my head I probably would have accepted that, as a couple, we were doomed, but I couldn't really think about it just then. Other than music,

Jan was my life. I had been with her since I was fifteen. I had started to shave, passed my school exams and degree as her boyfriend. I had bought my first proper album (*Selling England by the Pound* by Genesis) only weeks before we started going out, and she was the first and only person with whom I had had a proper sexual relationship. Together we had gone through pregnancy scares, illnesses, celebrations, depression and triumph. I just couldn't imagine not being with her.

No two days at the rehearsal studio were the same. We did more or less the same things, going through the songs, dissecting all the parts, making little changes here and there, working up to performing the entire set, but there were always other things going on.

Watching the comings and goings of other bands was a constant fascination. Bucks Fizz were encamped in one of the rooms for a week and we bumped into them outside if a break happened to coincide with theirs. The view from the alleyway outside the rehearsal rooms was not the most inspiring; a thick plait of railway lines led under a bridge close by and wove towards King's Cross Station a few hundred yards away, and grey slabs of council blocks lined up in the middle distance, but it was fun to talk to others in the business and I did what I think was a convincing job of sounding like an old pro mulling over the tour dates to come and the way the album had turned out.

But a lot of the time we only saw famous faces from a distance as they entered their rehearsal rooms or disappeared through the gates of the complex in long black cars. One morning Jan and I turned the corner at the entrance to the long, muddy alleyway that led to our block of rehearsal rooms and saw a row of four huge Harley Davidsons parked outside the rehearsal room next to ours. We edged our way along the alleyway; me in my Chinese slippers, carefully ripped clothes, wearing a beret and eye make-up, Jan in a black mini-skirt, leather jacket and plimsolls, her hair spiked up. Suddenly, as we passed the rehearsal room door next to ours, Midge Ure and the rest of Ultravox walked out dressed in tight leathers. Ignoring us completely, they paced over to the Harleys, kick-started them into ebullient life and roared off down the alleyway.

This was not so long after 'Vienna', Ultravox's biggest hit, and I was *très* impressed. 'Did you see who's next door?' I exclaimed as we walked into our rehearsal room.

Alannah was sitting on an amp, drawing hungrily on a cigarette, trying desperately to look like Bette Davis. 'Yeah, bunch of tossers,' she said and looked away.

Most of the time we all got on very well, and Alannah was the only one to strain relationships. She was naturally confrontational and seemed determined to dominate every situation. She criticised Joe's and Tom's dress sense remorselessly. To her, Joe's clothes were too slick, too 'Italian', whereas Tom was just shabby and had no idea how to present himself as a pop star. In some ways she was probably right. Joe did love his Italian loafers and silk shirts a little too much, and Tom was overly keen on his old blue trench-coat, bought in Camden Market when he first hit London a few years earlier, but it was the *way* she criticised rather than what she said that grated. She was always right, never to be questioned.

And Alannah did a convincing job of making you think she was brimming over with self-confidence. She knew exactly what she wanted and how to get it. Little more than a year after these rehearsals in Islington, she was asked by a journalist if she aspired to be as big as Duran Duran or Culture Club. 'Oh no . . . Much bigger, darling,' she replied, and she meant it.

Alannah was probably the one most violently set upon change. She wanted to throw off the shackles of the Twins' past, their sound, their look and the sort of fans they had once had. In many respects she felt slightly embarrassed by what they had done in the past and the people who had liked them. Tom merely saw the recent convulsions as a means to an end. 'Once,' he would say, 'it was enough to make music for our friends, for the few hundred people who were our fan base, but then we realised we could and should make music for the world. We want millions of people to like us.' And the Thompson Twins succeeded with this wish. Three years after Tom said this to me, they could look back upon sales of 25 million records. But Alannah was not content with this philosophy. She wanted to push things much further. Just before rehearsals began, she suggested the idea of having barbed wire stretched across the front of the stage at each concert – a complete reversal of the old approach of the original Twins, when members of the audience were welcomed on stage at the end of the show to play percussion and sing. When I first heard this idea I thought how ironic it was that the Thompson Twins' first album had been called *A Product of Participation.*

Another bright idea of Alannah's was to have three of us – Jan, Andrew and me – wearing latex masks so that we looked more like twins of Tom, Joe and her. She had the masks specially manufactured by an artist, a Joe mask for Andrew, an Alannah twin for Jan and a Tom Bailey rubber number for me. The problem was that Andrew couldn't see where he was going when he was wearing his mask, and during the first rehearsal with it he smashed the neck of his bass against an amp. Jan and I could hardly breathe and the masks itched terribly when they warmed up – and that was in a rehearsal room, not under the hot stage lights we would be using on the tour. Finally, Alannah had to concede defeat and, much to my relief, the masks were binned.

But when it came to music Alannah was not nearly so assertive, and for a lot of the time in rehearsals she was simply bored. Her role was organising the show, the look of the band, not its sound, and she could become impatient with the need to refine things musically. She was not a great singer, and when one (or sometimes all of us) pointed out that she was singing backing vocals so out of tune she could have been performing a different song, she was not a happy bunny. She would either insist she was in tune and everyone else was sharp or she would storm off in a cloud of expletives. In that way, the Thompson Twins were no different from any other band in rehearsal and in this respect, Jan and I were far from novices.

For my part, I tried to ignore her histrionics and concentrate on the music. And Tom was incredibly level-headed and calm. The strongest comment I ever heard him make during the rehearsals was after Alannah had gone off on a rant about something and he turned to her and said: 'Do you know, Alannah, sometimes you can be a very difficult person to live with.' That was Tom the music teacher coming out, I thought, as I watched from behind the Prophet V keyboard.

Tom and I became good friends during rehearsals. We understood one another very quickly and that understanding grew. He and I shared an ability to write songs and although he was far more successful than me, he appreciated the music I wrote and he was genuinely keen to be involved with the career of Colour-Me-Pop. He also loved Jan's voice and thought we had great potential as a two-piece. He and I shared similar tastes, enjoyed the same books, liked the same bands and ultimately had the same aspirations. I remember Alannah saying to me once that Tom would be completely content if he was locked in a room with just food and water and the means to record music. 'He could happily stay there for ever,' she said with more than a trace of envy. Jan could have said exactly the same of me.

During rehearsals we were trying to reproduce the songs on *Quick Step and Sidekick* note for note, but I couldn't resist experimenting a little by adding extra harmonies and the odd new melody, just to see if they worked. This annoyed Alannah and if she noticed anything different in the overall sound she would tell me not to mess around, but Tom, who, after all, had written everything we were playing, usually loved what I did and told me to keep it in next time.

My fondest memory from the time I was a member of the Thompson Twins was when, one morning a few weeks into rehearsals, we took a break from playing through the set and Tom came over to the keyboard.

'I really liked what you added to "Love On Your Side" just now,' Tom said. 'What was it?' And he walked up to the Prophet V and after a few seconds he duplicated what I had played. 'Yes, clever . . . very clever. I wish I'd thought of that when we were recording it.'

And suddenly I was a fan again and felt incredibly embarrassed. Tom came and sat on a large flight case standing next to the synth stand. 'When this tour is over,' he said, looking at me intently, 'you and I should go off together to write the next album. Go to Wales or something.'

I stared at him aghast. 'You serious?'

'Yeah, why not?'

'Well . . . fine,' I said. 'That would be brilliant.'

And with that he got up, smiled, patted me on the back and walked off towards the kitchen.

26

After much deliberation, the band and management had settled upon a second choice for the support band for the UK leg of the tour. A few months earlier, they had received a 12″ single entitled 'Pale Shelter' from a group called Tears for Fears. Alannah had wanted them from the off and claimed that 'Pale Shelter' was one of the best songs she had ever heard. The others – Joe, Tom and John Hade – had wanted Colour-Me-Pop. When we told them we couldn't do the tour, the Twins' management had contacted Tears for Fears.

In the interim, Tears for Fears had really taken off. 'Pale Shelter' had been an indie success and their second single, 'Mad World', had just entered the charts and was climbing steadily as word-of-mouth began to shift units. By the time their support was agreed, they were in the Top 20 and 'Lies', the Twins' first single in their new incarnation, had only just been released and was struggling to find a place in the Top 100.

Although the Thompson Twins and Tears for Fears would both become internationally successful, in the late summer of 1982, as we were preparing to begin the tour, there was an embarrassing disparity between the support band and the headlining act. The Twins had been around for years and were much better known in the music business, but they wanted to cast off their old image and considered themselves to be starting afresh, so for a time, all of us felt a little worried about the fact that Tears for Fears were apparently the better-known band.

People have often asked me how I feel about the fact that we could not make the support slot and Tears for Fears did, and then went on to become multi-millionaires and globally famous. They are often surprised when I just shrug and say it was 'one of those things'. But, the fact is, we were not in a position to go on a tour. We had no real band, our old bassist, Martin, probably wouldn't have given up his plans for a Master's degree and our drummer, Colin, would not have left his job; but most importantly, we had no backing. I had created an opening for us with the *Europe in the Year Zero* EP almost by default, whereas Tears for Fears were with a proper record label and had the financial support to give them the lift they needed. Also, they were successful in their own right before supporting the Twins; it wasn't the support tour that propelled them into pop stardom. For every band like Tears for Fears there are probably hundreds who go on the road to support a famous group and still get nowhere.

Rehearsals continued pretty much as they had begun. Within two weeks we could play through the set almost perfectly and after that it was just a question of practising until we could play the songs on auto-pilot while retaining a feel for the music – which is actually a rather difficult trick to pull off.

People dropped into the rehearsal room from time to time. We saw a lot of John, who was updating us all on the tour details. The dates had been finalised and advanced sales were going well. During one particular visit he sat us all down and gave us a lecture on the dangers of visiting the States.

'The hookers on 42nd Street,' he said with exaggerated seriousness, 'just grab you by the balls and ask you if you fancy a good time.'

'And God knows what they say to men,' I quipped. Everyone laughed except John, who gave me a stern look.

'Listen, this is serious,' he went on. 'New York in particular is not nice. Girls have been snatched, kept for days in cellars without food or water and raped repeatedly. The drugs are often bad – it's not unusual to get Ajax mixed in with coke. And then there's herpes – it's now almost an epidemic. You'll have to be very careful.'

On another occasion John brought along an A & R man from Arista. Tom introduced me to him, and as soon as I saw him I recognised his face. I had been in his office with our latest recordings just a few weeks before meeting John Hade. He did not remember me of course – I was one of a cast of thousands who traipsed through his life trying to sell him something he didn't want.

That afternoon he was a very different man from the person I had played our tape to, he actually wanted to talk to me, asked me how I was finding rehearsals and living in London. He even had the cheek to say that he had heard some snatches of Colour-Me-Pop and suggested that Jan and I call in to see him with John sometime during or after the tour. I would like to tell you I asked him to kiss my arse, but I didn't. I smiled, made all the right noises and said it would be a pleasure.

We rehearsed five days a week every week, but we had the weekends to ourselves. On the third weekend Tom and I went shopping. We had been instructed by Alannah to spend the day buying clothes for the tour. These were not stage clothes (those were put together by another designer friend of John's) but clothes for us to wear off-stage, on the road and most importantly at parties and public events. Alannah rightly knew that the image of a pop group was a twenty-four-seven thing and that we were always to play a role wherever we were.

After meeting up at John's house Tom and I were each handed an envelope. It bulged alluringly. I opened mine and with growing amazement I counted twenty fifty-pound notes, one thousand pounds . . . it was almost what I had to live on for a year as a student. Tom had the same and nonchalantly stuffed the envelope in his pocket. Then he and I headed out the door as Alannah and Jan got themselves ready to go out with their own bundles of cash.

We headed in a black cab straight for South Molton Street, off Oxford Street. There the shops were filled with what I thought were unbelievably expensive clothes, shirts for £100, £300 suits, and shoes that cost a month's worth of grant cheque. And I just froze – I went into spending paralysis, unable to buy anything I saw.

Part of the problem was Tom; he had no interest in expensive clothes. He had a distinctive style, as I suppose I did, but it had nothing to do with these sort of shops. The fact was that I had never had any money; from when I first became interested in fashion I had created my own style from Oxfam suits and clothes bought at jumble sales. Tom was the same; sudden wealth, even if it had been loaned by the record company, was a strange new concept to him. Ten years later, by which time I had entered my designer clothes stage, I would have been delighted to blow £1,000 of someone else's money in South Molton Street and I did buy suits that had then risen to £500 a throw; but in 1982, such attractions were utterly lost on me.

Tom and I wandered along the arcades and the bustling streets. London seemed to be awakening from a slumber. The stores were packed, new emporia selling all things expensive and 'designer' were springing up and there was an atmosphere of hope, a definable sense of expectation in the air. The country had just emerged triumphant from the Falklands War. The public had made the deliberate choice to ignore what the war had meant, the role our leaders had played and what their motivations had been; all that would creep into our collective conscience later. Now, the early autumn sun was shining and the world seemed a benign place. These were the days I had dreamed about for so long. At that very moment I was living the rock 'n' roll fantasy. I was walking through London streets with Tom Bailey, we had red spiky hair and we looked like twins, heads turned. Life, I thought, didn't get much better than this.

We stopped for coffee in Covent Garden and began to talk about our pasts, our present, our hopes and aspirations. I asked Tom about Alannah.

'Things are a bit, you know, chaotic at the moment.'

'But you are a couple?'

'Unofficially.'

'A-ha.'

'Alannah thinks we should be seen as single . . . Sells more records.'

I was gobsmacked. 'Yeah, if you're the fucking Bay City Rollers!'

Tom just shrugged. 'No, she's probably right. Anyway, it's just a game. It doesn't really affect anything in real life.'

But I could tell there was a lot more to this story; beneath the surface acceptance lay a well of sadness.

'We have a sort of loose relationship,' he went on. 'It's best that way.'

And suddenly I could see it all. It seemed to me that Tom, older than Alannah by some five years, was more serious about their relationship, he wanted stability as well as fame, but Alannah was not there yet, she needed space and time. She wanted to play the pop star and the post-feminist, to live as she liked but to keep a loose relationship with Tom. Which was fine, if they both wanted it.

'What about you and Jan?' Tom asked, staring into my eyes.

'Oh,' I said, looking away for a moment. 'It's been better.'

'You've been together a long time though, right?'

'Seven years,' I said, and Tom whistled.

'I like to think we're okay, but this summer has put us into a chaotic state too. I don't know if we'll be able to settle back the way we were when things calm down. I hope so, but, you know . . .'

We ended up at a shop called Flip, an American retro store that specialised in low-price '60s clothes and new designs that were slightly off the wall. Jauntily, having had a fantastic day out, Tom and I returned to Clapham with three brightly-coloured cotton shirts each from Flip, total price: £6.

27

Alannah hit the roof. Of course, she and Jan had experienced little difficulty in spending their money, and each had returned to John's house laden down with dozens of bags and boxes. The following Saturday Tom was marched off to Knightsbridge with Alannah and I was sent into town with Joe, to make sure we got the right sort of stuff this time.

Joe was really into fashion. His style was not to Alannah's liking but she had given him explicit instructions about what to buy, and he could be trusted to spend £1,000 in no time at all. It turned into a whirlwind shop, in and out of changing rooms with huge piles of clothes to try on. One particular store that sticks in my mind was a shoe shop near Oxford Circus called World of Mud. It was one of the earliest theme shops in London. As the door shut behind us the sound of traffic suddenly disappeared and we were transported into a dreamscape, a cave with stalactites hanging low from the ceiling, a spiral staircase that led to the upper floor, and beside the steps a bubbling mud pool. It was more like some- thing out of Disneyland than a shop, and at first I had trouble spotting what the place sold. But then I noticed, dotted around the walls, little alcoves cut into the fake rock in which were placed single pairs of shoes. I picked up a boot and felt the incredibly soft leather, turned it over in my hand and checked the price tag before gingerly placing it back in its personal cubby-hole.

It was Joe's favourite shop of the moment, and when we left half an hour later he was in high spirits having bought two pairs of staggeringly expensive boots.

Joe was a tremendous person to shop with. He knew every expensive boutique in Central London and spoke with authority about each. He was very different to Tom and slightly detached from the whole Thompson Twins carousel. He loved being in the band, of course, but he saw his role as almost exclusively theatrical and he would really only come into his own when we hit the tour full-on a few short weeks later. He had loved acting but knew the Thompson Twins' blend of theatre and music would prove far more exciting for him.

I never saw Joe perform in a play or on film, but I imagine he was a fine actor. When I asked him about it, he said that he had appeared in a handful of modern interpretations of Shakespeare, and suddenly as we crossed a street he slipped into a soliloquy from *Henry V*. Reaching the pavement, he began reciting sonnets and set-pieces from his favourites, totally oblivious to the staring passers-by.

This time Alannah was satisfied with the shopping trip, and I must say it felt great putting my limited selection of old clothes in a bag at the house and to start wearing the things we'd bought.

Soon after this we hit a really hectic spell. Andrew offered

Jan and me a room in his house in Clapham (he lived around the corner from Tom, Alannah and John). We liked the house in Highgate, but we thought we would feel closer to the centre of things if we moved to Clapham. Luckily, the car was repaired the weekend of the big shop and the next day, a Sunday, we said our farewells to the designer and her family and packed the Vauxhall Viva with the half-dozen bags and boxes that constituted almost all our possessions and drove down to Clapham to settle in Andrew's spare room in a large house close to Clapham Common, a two-minute walk from the others.

During the following week we had some respite from rehearsals, but we had no time to relax. John had been contacted by the Musicians' Union who wanted to send an inspector along to the studio to check the recording of the next single, 'Love On Your Side'.

When John met us at a rehearsal and said that we had to be inspected in the studio the next day, I looked at him totally bemused. 'What do you mean, inspected?' I asked.

'Oh, it's a lot of crap,' Tom interjected. 'The Musicians' Union send out inspectors to check we're not using semi-pro musicians and under-paying them. They also have a real problem with too many synthesisers and drum machines – technology is supposed to be damaging the livelihoods of so called "real musicians".'

I had heard about all this vaguely from articles in the *NME* but I couldn't believe the Union actually checked up on people.

'It's just our bad luck they picked us,' John added. 'But unless we agree to the inspection they won't sanction the record and it won't be played on the radio, so we're over a barrel.'

Next morning we all appeared at The Point in Victoria, a studio partly owned by the Twins. The inspector, a weaselly little man in an ill-fitting suit, arrived early and sat in the mixing room as we went through the process of 'recording' 'Love On Your Side'. We just performed it very hurriedly and the engineer submitted it to tape almost live. Then, while John distracted the inspector, the engineer surreptitiously switched the newly recorded tape for the original version recorded in the Caribbean and at Rak, a process that had taken weeks to perfect.

The Point was a lovely little studio, a million times better than anything I had used, but not in the same league as Rak. During a break in the fake recording I was wandering around and in a back room I stumbled across an old Hammond organ. Just as I was looking at it appreciatively one of the engineers came in.

'That's the very organ used on "House Of The Rising Sun",' he remarked before collecting something and leaving again. I sat down and switched on the Hammond, touched a few keys and revelled in the fantastic sound only these beautiful instruments can produce. Then, looking round to make sure there was no one about, I started playing the chords to the famous song that had been recorded on this very instrument: A-minor, C, D . . . It felt amazing to be here, now, playing one of the songs Jan and I used to churn out in Southend wine bars a few years earlier.

The recording of 'Love On Your Side' took only a couple of hours and it amazed and amused me to think the inspector was gullible enough to believe a single could be polished off like that. I knew the Musicians' Union played a useful role but I couldn't believe they were so backward in their thinking. Thankfully, things have changed enormously since then.

John drove Jan and me back to Clapham. On the way he had to stop near Victoria Station to pick up some documents from an office just off Victoria Street. We all jumped out the car and he searched for some change for the meter.

'Do either of you have twenty pence?' he asked. Neither of us had.

'Oh fuck it,' he exclaimed and marched off.

We headed for the office, Jan and I trying to keep up with him as he strode along the street.

Ten minutes later we were back at the car and found the inevitable parking ticket on the windscreen. John said nothing, just snatched it from the glass, walked round to the boot and tossed it in. As the lid of the boot closed I caught a glimpse of a pile of similar tickets.

'Another one for the collection,' he said straight-faced as we piled back into the car.

'Don't you care?' I asked.

'Nah!' he replied with a grin. 'I'm going to be fucking rich in a few months.'

The sickening thing is: the bastard was too.

28

This period feels now to have been a time in limbo, exciting but at the same time incredibly disjointed.

One evening towards the end of our preparation for the tour, we had finished rehearsing at about 6 P.M. and a few minutes later John arrived with a TV, a VCR, and, clutched proudly in his hand, the test edit of the band's first video, for the single 'Lies'.

John set up the TV and tape machine and we all clustered together to watch the video. It had been shot before any of us new members had joined and featured just Tom, Joe and Alannah. I saw it again recently and it looks incredibly dated, as though it had been found buried in a time capsule deposited there perhaps a century ago in a box along with a turntable, a CB radio and an episode of *Blake's Seven*. But on that cold early October evening it gave us all a huge thrill. Tom was more than a little embarrassed by it, Alannah kept criticising his and Joe's moves and saying how awful she looked, but the very thought that this would hopefully appear on *Top of the Pops* soon gave us a real buzz. In fact, it never was shown on *TOTP* because 'Lies' failed to enter even the Top 50 and success for the Twins came first with the follow-up single, but that does nothing to tarnish the memory.

Then the incongruity. John shot off to a meeting somewhere, Andrew and Boris left for a party thrown by some close friends and Tom, Joe, Alannah, Jan and I all piled into the Vauxhall Viva rusting before our eyes outside the rehearsal room.

I can still see in memory the Marylebone Road flying past and in the rear-view mirror catching a glimpse of the three original Twins sitting cramped together in the back, all hair and bright clothes. I had to stop for petrol in an underground garage near Great Portland Street and stood in the cold, misty night pumping gas into the car, shivering and growing increasingly aware that wet air and cold do nothing for gelled hair.

Then we were back in pop-star mode as we arrived at our destination, the studio of the clothes designer who had created our stage outfits. It was in a basement off Bedford Square in Bloomsbury, and exotic clothes were draped from hangers and doors throughout the couple of tiny rooms. Three weeks earlier the designer had taken our measurements and Tom and I had been staggered to learn that his measurements and mine were absolutely identical. The designer had joked that maybe we really were long-lost twins after all.

We tried on the clothes, originally conceived by Alannah. Each of us wore grey suits. The trousers were calf length and the jackets had small lapels. Under the jackets we wore crisp white shirts and black ties. The effect was completed with identical Ray-Ban sunglasses. When Tom and I stood facing each other we looked like reflections; it was quite bizarre.

An hour later we were back in Clapham, exhausted. 'Tomorrow,' Tom reminded us, as we dropped him and Alannah off at their house, 'is the big day, remember . . . the final dress rehearsal.'

I had completely forgotten. And despite having rehearsed to death during the past six weeks, I felt a tremor of fear at the prospect.

29

It was just like being a little kid again, when the tooth fairies have done their work. The music fairies, the road crew, had been busy through the night. We had left the rehearsal room just as it had been for weeks, a mess of instruments, leads and general detritus. When we arrived at ten o'clock on the final Friday of rehearsals, the room had been transformed.

Across the width of the room, the road crew had created a mock stage set. There was a huge white backdrop and in front of that, two screens, one about eight feet tall in the centre made of paper supported by a metal outer frame, and to stage right, a screen about four feet high behind which the keyboards stood. To the other side of the large screen was the drum rostrum, and in front of this, places for Tom in the middle and Joe and Alannah to each side.

And there was a tangible air of expectancy very different from a normal rehearsal day. A wardrobe lady had set up shop in a little room off the kitchen. She had our stage clothes crisply ironed with name tags on them. It was like being back at school. The lighting engineers had set up an array of lights pointed at the stage and the sound crew were adjusting microphones and untangling leads.

And all this grandeur made me nervous. I knew the songs as though they had been the mantra to my life, and I had rehearsed the set a thousand times, but what made me anxious was the fact that this would be the first time we had played before an audience – the management, publishing executives and most importantly the record company bosses had all been invited to see what they had been paying for.

By eleven, everyone was there and we were in our stage clothes. The record company guys were last to arrive. John met them at the door. An A & R guy had brought along a colleague from the London office and two from New York who happened to be in London that week. The wardrobe lady, Joan, who would be on the tour with us was just applying some colour to my cheeks when I saw the suits arrive. Tom was out in the rehearsal room and everyone was shaking hands, then John led them through to the kitchen, Mr A & R gave me a brief nod and then John showed them all where the toilet was located before coming back into the kitchen. At first I thought it was an odd coincidence that four men all wanted to use the loo at the same moment, and then the penny dropped. I looked at John, tapped my nose and raised my eyebrows. He just gave me a wry smile and headed back out to the rehearsal room. A few minutes later Joan was finished with me, I checked how I looked in the mirror by the kitchen door and walked out . . . And straight into one of the execs from the Big Apple, emerging first of the four from the toilet. I looked at him and apologised and he gave me a huge smile and patted me on the back. I chose not to mention he had a line of blood pirouetting out of his left nostril and

turned towards the main room where the others were
assembled.

It all went amazingly well. I made a couple of little mistakes
and Alannah hit a few bum notes but overall, from where I
stood, it sounded great. It was also the first time we had
tried out many of the theatrical props.

Joe and Alannah had created some really cool set-pieces.
Those that stand out in my mind came towards the end of
the show. There was a song called 'All Fall Out', a slow,
brooding song with a mechanical beat that sounded like a
steam engine. For this Alannah stood behind the large screen
and messed around with a mocked-up machine made of
painted wood. Inside was a canister that squirted dry ice
through a hole in the top of the machine. During the song,
Alannah hit a timpani drum standing beside the steam
machine and every so often released the steam. All the while
she was back-lit by a spotlight behind her. From the audience
this looked incredible: Alannah looked about ten feet tall and
appeared to be controlling a huge steam generator which she
hit periodically.

The other set-piece came later, after the screen had been
used to project an assortment of images. Andrew stood
behind the huge paper screen at the start of the last song and
at an appropriate moment he burst straight through it on to
the stage all the while playing a thumping bass line. Unlike
the cocoons in *Spinal Tap*, it worked beautifully.

When the show was over, the audience of a dozen or so
burst into enthusiastic applause and we all went out front to
be congratulated and to have hands shaken. The only people
keeping to themselves were the sound and lighting crews
who were even then going through the post-mortem of the
show and complaining about their own mistakes, about feed-
back and cross-parallax, top-end distortion and focal-length
incompatibilities.

I did my share of smiling and accepting praise but managed to slip away as the champagne corks began to pop. Outside it was freezing and I was worried about muddying my stage clothes, but I felt that I had to get away for a few minutes. After the stage lights and the glitz, Islington looked especially drab. The trains were passing beneath the nearby bridge as usual, the grey council towers glowered malevolently, just as they always did, and I could hear a distant thump from a neighbouring rehearsal room where some famous but invisible pop group were working out their set.

So this was it then, I thought. Everything was ready, all things prepared, the engine revved, the sap risen. The tour would begin on Tuesday; first date, Reading University. And as I watched my warm breath in the cold air I couldn't decide whether what I was then feeling was over-excitement or just sheer terror. We live in interesting times, I thought, and headed, shivering, back to the rehearsal room and the waiting champagne glass.

30

When I was a child I used to play a game in which I could project myself into the future. If something unpleasant had been planned, like a dentist appointment or if I had to read an essay to the class, I would imagine it was all over and I was through the other side. In another game I imagined time slowing down so that the bad moment might never come – I would slow down and listen to the seconds thundering in my ears – dong, dong . . . dong . . . . . . dong.

It didn't work, of course: the dentist was always there with the drill and the smirks of my classmates never differed. And when I came through the other side? Well, there were just other things to fear, new dreads to find ways round. And so, on 19 October 1982, I sat alone in my stage suit and thin black tie, Ray-Bans in my hand in the loo backstage at Reading University, feeling sick and trying to slow the seconds.

Outside I could hear the between-bands disco playing 'Hungry Like The Wolf' by Duran Duran followed by that horrible song by Musical Youth. Behind the music, the hum of the crowd, a thousand students filling the main hall. Closer, the sounds of the road crew, the rumble of a flight-case wheeled along a corridor; Jeff, the lighting engineer, telling someone to 'get a fucking move on'. Then once, from the stage, the 'phatt' of a synth keyboard being tested for level.

I kept trying to reassure myself I'd been through this hundreds of times before. Okay, the stage was bigger, the audience five times the size of any I had performed in front of before, but this would be no lame Watch With Mother effort playing in a seedy club for fifty drunks. The Thompson Twins were adored by students – at least the old Twins had been, and the audience would be with us all the way – they were there for a good night out. Nothing to worry about.

I ran through the set again in my mind. There were bits I dreaded. The opening chords of 'In The Name Of Love' always terrified me. It was the band's most famous song and the opening motif was instantly recognisable, a slight slip of the finger and it would sound unbelievably horrible . . . My God! My fingers, I thought, they've gone stiff, I can't move them! I looked at them, mortified.

The panic was wheeling up, churning inside. I took deep breaths and looked around for something that would bring me back into focus. On the back of the toilet door some graffiti. 'Yesterday I didn't know how to spell engineer, now I are one,' I read. And another, just above the toilet-roll dispenser: 'English degrees, please take one.' That felt better. I put on my Ray-Bans, studied the dark ceiling and took another deep breath. Then I stood up, left the cubicle and walked across the room to the mirror. There I was in my Thompson Twins uniform, transformed by the passing of three months. And I thought the change was cool. 'For fuck's sake! My life is

cool . . . Everything is cool,' I shouted to myself. Six months
ago I would have been in a similar audience. Now I was in a
famous band about to play to them.

'It will be okay,' I said quietly to my reflection. 'I can do
this.' Turning, I strode to the door and the over-lit corridor
beyond.

I remember nothing of that gig, except that after the final
note faded away and the audience roared their approval, I ran
off stage with the others waving to the crowd and feeling
more relieved than I had ever felt about anything in my life,
even the dentist.

There is sometimes an amazing feeling of camaraderie
between members of a band, especially during moments of
triumph. We were all elated that night. I even remember
hugging Alannah, feeling her wet face against mine and
catching a few strands of her hair in my mouth. For that
moment, we were almost friends. Over-excited and hyper,
we felt like soldiers after a night raid, surprised and joyous
our bodies were whole, our limbs intact.

And of course we celebrated. Some old fans from long-lost
tours were there and I was introduced to the national fan-
club co-ordinator, a devotee from 1979. Tears for Fears
joined us and we each toasted one another's successful performances. They seemed perfectly relaxed and at ease, in
spite of the fact that they had played only a handful of gigs in
their careers, but then they were at Number 12 in the chart
that week, the bastards.

It was the sort of evening when everyone was likeable. I
remember jamming on an old honky-tonk piano with Roland
Orzabal, the tubby one from Tears for Fears, and drinking
slammers with Curt Smith, the tall one with long plaited
hair. After that first gig I decided I really liked Curt – he was
open and modest – whereas I thought Roland was a little too
proud of himself.

The buzz we got from the gig kept us all awake long into the morning – we knew we could sleep on the bus the next day. But gradually, the hangers-on drifted away and at about 4 A.M. John suggested we get on the tour bus and head back to the hotel.

But even then I couldn't sleep. And as Jan curled up under the duvet I stood at the window of the hotel room listening to the hum of the air-conditioning and watching the light break over the concrete hills and the fields of plexiglas.

'This feels good,' I decided. 'Yes, I can cope with this. Being a pop star is not at all bad.'

31

Despite what you read about the hedonism, the drugs and the mayhem, there is a certain rhythm to the life of a band on tour.

For sure, we became creatures of the night. The daytime was for travelling from one city to another on the tour bus and often, even though we were exhausted and had gone without sleep, we still could not rest. There were eight of us on a thirty-seater coach, so if any of us felt unhappy there were plenty of places in which we could sit alone to sulk. But most of the time we all got on remarkably well. And, far from the image bands like to convey to the press, we all did rather boring things on the bus. We read books, watched videos, played the primitive computer games then available, Space Invaders and PacMan. And when the technology got too much, we resorted to Travel Scrabble and chess – wild!

Coach time was our 'being normal' time, as I know it is for

almost all bands on the road. It is the time when no one but
the band and the crew can observe you, a time when there are
no uninvited photographers, film crews, or fans. A private
time. It was only off the coach that the world was a very different place.

John Lennon once said that a tour is a room, a car, a plane,
a room, and that is pretty accurate. The routine went something like this: leave a place about 10 A.M. Stop for lunch on
the motorway and arrive at the next venue around 2 P.M. The
crew would have left the night before immediately after the
previous show or early that morning and the stage set and
gear would be arranged by the time we arrived. As we
trooped in the sound guys would be yelling down microphones, 'One two, one two . . . cliché, cliché.' And the lights
would be flashing randomly. Either Jeff, the lighting engineer, or his assistant would be dangling from a gantry above
the stage sorting out wires. Tony, one of the roadies, might
be spotted stage left shaking an amp in an effort to fix a
highly technical fault or wrapping an enormous length of
cable around his arm using his elbow as a grip. A sound man
would be shouting instructions to someone on the stage; the
wardrobe lady, Joan, worked alone unpacking costumes and
the manager of the venue stood in discussion with John
about the rider – the list of requirements for all of us, things
ranging from precise brands of mineral water to the nature of
the sandwich fillings.

We had nothing else to do but to sit around twiddling our
thumbs. None of us could leave the building because we had
no idea when the sound-check would be or if there were
problems that we needed to advise with, so it was just a question of filling in the time. Once in while, when it was obvious
nothing would happen for two hours or we had arrived early,
we could escape to look around wherever we happened to be.

Later each day there was the sound-check. The first time
we did one, at Reading, it was an exciting novelty, and the

second, in Folkestone, was far from humdrum, but by about the fifth or sixth date of the tour, testing one's keyboard and mic for level had become tedious, a necessary chore.

And the evening often came slowly. After the sound-checks there was invariably more sitting around nibbling sandwiches and drinking gallons of strong coffee, popping tabs of speed to keep awake because the wave of tiredness from the 4 A.M. game of pool was finally hitting. Then suddenly the tempo would change. The venue would open around 7.30 or 8. The disco started up, the place began to fill and this massive buzz would build. A typical page of the tour itinerary reads: Norwich to Coventry, 150 miles. Staying at Beechwood Hotel. Venue: Main Hall, Coventry Polytechnic. Capacity of Hall: 970. Stage Size: 21 × 20. Equipment Arrives: 10 A.M. Sound Check: 3.30 P.M. Doors Open: 8 P.M. On Stage: 10.30 P.M.

Most nights, Tears for Fears would take the stage about nine and I would usually watch them from out front with one of the others, often Tom or Andrew. I thought they were brilliant, even after a dozen or so gigs. They were an extremely polished and professional band and I liked their songs very much. Like the Thompson Twins, they were then hitting a steep ascendant and they knew it and understandably revelled in it. I admired them and liked the fact that they never once said anything about our chart debut not doing quite as well as theirs.

By the seventh gig, at Rock City in Nottingham, the members of the two bands had become good friends, sharing both the boredom and the highs. That afternoon, the new chart appeared and we heard in the dressing room after the sound check that Tears for Fears had sold 33,000 copies of 'Mad World' that day alone, and that the single was now at Number 3. We also heard that 'Lies' had fallen out of the Top 100.

*

It was around this time that my relatively innocent flirtation
with drugs became more serious. Although I thought I had
been around, until I went on tour and started earning decent
money I was actually pretty inexperienced with pharmaceuticals. I had been smoking dope since my teens, but rarely kept
any in the flat, and a couple of years earlier Tim and I had
experimented with some acid he'd somehow managed to pro-
cure. The big drug for the professional musician though,
then, as now, was cocaine – often referred to as 'white T-shirt'.
As a student I could hardly have blown a week's worth of
grant cheque on a line of the stuff, even if I'd wanted to, and
I only knew a couple of people who had tried it. Now though,
I was on tour with a professional band, and all I had to do to
earn a fortnight's worth of grant cheque in a day was to dance
around and play a few songs each night. I had a bit of money
for a change, I was in showbiz proper, and trying a line of
coke seemed the obvious next step. And besides, I've always
had a will with the breaking strain of a Mars bar.

But for some reason I didn't want anyone else to know of
my decision and so I contacted a dealer myself. After a great
gig at Rock City I met the guy in an empty back room of the
venue. He looked a little rough around the edges but you
wouldn't have given him a second glance on the street. He
locked the door, took out a small clear plastic packet from an
inside pocket and laid out the white powder on a faded
mirror he told me he always carried with him. I looked at the
cocaine with a blend of fear and excitement. It was just so
white, so fine, so fucking cool-looking, how could I not be
seduced by it? Suddenly I had a rolled-up £10 note in my
hand and I was leaning towards the mirror.

'Just draw it up and move the note along as you do it,' I
was told.

Other than it enhancing my long-term memory for the
events of the next few hours, that first line of cocaine actually did very little for me. I have a vivid picture of the band

that night. After the gig we were all starving and someone decided we should go for a curry. Curt, Roland and the rest of Tears for Fears decided to join us and we all headed to what was supposed to be the best Indian restaurant in the county. We found a table for fifteen and tucked into a mountain of poppadoms. I remember thinking that time was moving very fast and how attractive the wallpaper was. The curry seemed flavourless, but the tap water I kept ordering was really nice. And so it went on: Coventry, Bristol, Leicester, Norwich. They all now merge into one; a room, a car, a plane, a room, the same routine, the games on the coach, the sound-checks, the sandwich fillings.

That is, until Sheffield, when everything changed.

I don't know how long Jan had been awake. Maybe she hadn't been asleep at all and had just been laying there thinking and wondering what to say, wondering how she should put it. If she had, it was time wasted, because when she had decided what to say it all came out rather clumsily.

'You're still awake,' I said, sitting up. A street light through red curtains cast a pallid aura around everything in the room. Jan's face looked like a bird's. 'Mike. I'm in love with John,' she said.

I looked at her blankly.

'We're over. I want to be with John.'

I felt sick instantly. Nothing I could say seemed right for me or for her.

'I'm sorry,' she added, her voice a crisp monotone. She looked away.

'How long? What have you . . .?'

She turned. 'Nothing has happened. I just, I just know I love him.'

My mind raced through recent days. Last night had been a disastrous gig. There had been fewer than a hundred people in the 1,300-capacity Lyceum, and this was the band's home town. The sound was awful, it had been freezing in the venue and as we sweated under the lights, the perspiration soaked through so we were shivering when we left the stage, thoroughly miserable.

At the hotel, little more than an over-sized guest house with filthy carpets and a manageress with a fag dangling from the corner of her mouth, we had all tried to cover our pain in different ways. I had drunk too much, Joe and Alannah had disappeared to one of their rooms and Tom had played endless games of pool with Boris and Andrew, each of them studiously avoiding the subject of the show. Around one in the morning I had stumbled up the stairs leaving Jan, John and few of the others at the bar, where the manageress was mouthing off about Billy fucking Fury or someone.

And now it was all too perfect, a scriptwriter could hardly have wished for more. In the lobby and then outside, all around, the miserable faded squalor of the hotel, the hangovers and red eyes, the freezing pavement and the dog turd by the hotel door stuck to the concrete with tendrils of ice. And now I could feel my own personal, internal icicles, the permafrost nibbling into my guts.

The journey to Manchester was a haze of red-brick buildings, blurred cars and lorries, dirty sleet and grey. We were playing the Hacienda, then the coolest club in the country, a place I had only dreamed of playing, and I felt nothing. We went through the usual routine, but this time I felt enclosed within myself, I could hardly speak and made it my mission to avoid being within twenty feet of either John or Jan. Throughout the coach journey Jan had sat next to him, almost as a symbolic gesture. I felt like a cuckolded tribesman after my woman had moved to the chief's tent. I had caught the odd furtive glance from John but had looked away.

After that night we had four more dates to play, culminating in the showcase gig in London, but it was obvious I couldn't go on like this until then. Someone had to realise something was up and I didn't want to talk until somebody asked me what was wrong.

The right moment came just before we were due to go on stage at the Hacienda. I was in the dressing room with Tom and one of the roadies. This guy had rolled a joint, but as he was about to light it, we heard one of the crew calling him. As he headed out the door he threw the joint to me. 'Here,' he said, 'have it, Mike. Looks like you need it more than me.' I said nothing, but with exaggerated movements I struck a match and lit the spliff, ignoring Tom, concentrating on what I was doing as if I was performing open-heart surgery. But after a few puffs, a new wave of depression hit me like a truck and I threw the joint on to the floor, stamping on it. I looked at Tom's stunned expression.

'What's wrong?' he asked.

I avoided his gaze but wanted desperately to tell him. I listened for the sound of anyone approaching the dressing room, knowing that any second someone was bound to run in.

'Come on, Mike. What is it?'

'I can't . . .' I ran out of breath and must have looked totally lost. Somehow I managed to find some words. 'John and Jan . . .' I spluttered. 'John and Jan. They . . .'

'Oh fucking hell!' Tom stood up. 'Shit, no!' He ran his hands through his hair and turned around, then sat down again, dragging his chair closer to mine. He put a hand on my shoulder. 'I'm sorry,' he said with supreme gentleness. But I saw him look away, his face was pale with anxiety.

I was about to say something when the door opened. We both looked up and Jan came in. She looked at us, then away, strode to a table, picked something up and was in the corridor again all within the space of a few seconds. Outside, the last notes of Tears for Fears' encore, 'Mad World', resonated around the hall and the applause rose to a crescendo. We were due on stage in ten minutes.

32

I have to confess that I fell into a rather pathetic state. I managed to function as a musician, just; but that was about all. I should have realised that the allure of cannabis and cocaine was fake, that they would only make me feel worse. But self-pity is all-powerful, and the worse you make yourself feel physically, the more you seem to find liberation from emotion.

At least that's the idea. It's nonsense of course, merely a chimera and a potentially deadly one at that. Just say 'no', kids.

Needless to say, for the remainder of the tour I said 'yes'. I ate nothing, drank too much, started smoking cigarettes; another thank-you to Alannah for that, although of course, I only had myself to blame: I was big enough and old enough to know what I was doing.

At Brown's restaurant in Brighton, the lunchtime before

what turned out to be the best gig I ever played with the band, I embarrassed everyone, but most especially myself, by throwing up, not once, but twice. During the sound-check at Bath University I was so convinced I could see a pair of dogs chasing one another in a rabid blur in the middle of the hall that I only heard the sound engineer calling to me after Jan had dug me in the ribs with unnecessary force. That night I again embarrassed everyone, but most especially myself, when I decided to throw myself upon the (admittedly gorgeous) girlfriend of the band's agent, Andy Wolliscroft, and Tom had to guide me gently back to the hotel before I ended up in the A & E department of Bath's Royal United Hospital.

But, of course, although I couldn't spare a thought for anyone else at the time, I wasn't the only one going through the ringer. Tom was horrified by the turn of events and seething with John. They had been friends back in Sheffield, long before the band had started. They had been through privations together and now, just as everything was coming together, John's *amour* was threatening to mess it all up.

Tom and John had certainly had a little 'chat' soon after the Manchester gig and even I could detect a certain frostiness between them. It was only later that I realised why the band's agent had travelled down to Bath.

Jan became remote. We did not speak to each other for days after leaving the hotel room in Sheffield, and standing next to her at a keyboard on stage with the band each night was one of the oddest experiences of my life.

And Janet and John's relationship seemed to flourish in the face of everyone's anger. For me the most agonising aspect of the whole thing was the entrapment. When couples break up they usually keep away from one another completely; one of them leaves the home they once shared, or at least stop going to the same pub. But we could not leave the tour we once shared: 'a room, a car, a plane, a room' is a very small world and I saw Jan and John together most of the day. How could I avoid them? John used to do his job alone and with clinical efficiency, now Jan was nearly always beside him, swapping video games and Scrabble for helping out 'the management'.

Brown's in Brighton was definitely one of the low points, but a few hours later the band's performance at Top Rank was just stunning. It had begun well, with five hundred fans turned away at the door, and by eight that night the hall was heaving with bodies. Tears for Fears did not support us for that gig, they had to fly to Germany to pick up an award; instead, a solo artist called Black played in their place. He was extremely professional, but I was just not in the mood for his charismatic melancholia and could have done with a hefty dose of 'Mad World'. But in spite of the doom-laden mood hanging over the band, for some reason that night we all performed like demons.

Just before the tour I had finally persuaded Alannah to let me play guitar on one song in the set called 'Beach Culture'. I had worked out some funky chords, sort of Orange Juice meets James Brown, and I'd tried it in rehearsals. Tom loved it but Alannah had a pathological hatred for guitars. I wouldn't let it go, and finally she had caved. But somehow, when the tour started, there had been one hitch after another that stopped me playing guitar. One night the road crew discovered they had left my guitar at the previous night's venue, on another night my amp mysteriously malfunctioned during the sound-check, and it was not until the fifth date of the tour, in Coventry, that I had finally managed to get my way. Now, each night, the highlight of the show for me was to pick up my trusty Fender Telecaster and to run out from behind the keyboard plinth and jump around the stage with Tom playing my funky chords.

In Brighton, as in all the places where I had played guitar, the audience had loved it, mainly I think because they

thought we were going to start playing some old Thompson
Twins material (which was probably why Alannah was so
against it in the first place). After the show we had over two
hundred fans wanting autographs and I had my own little
crowd who spent an hour with me asking for mine. I signed
a dozen arms and an orange someone produced from a bag.
They all claimed they loved the new band but wondered why
we didn't use more guitar. It wasn't for me to explain.

It had been a wonderful, if temporary, tonic. Just when my
self-esteem was at its lowest point I was receiving adulation,
and whenever in later years I gave any thought to what might
have happened if I had stayed with the band, I cast my mind
back to that night and that hour with those kids hanging on
my every word, desperate to have a part of me, to be me.
Only a few months earlier I had wanted to be Andy Gill of
the Gang of Four.

Of course the high you get from being an object of desire
is irresistible. That's why people become addicted to fame; it
is a potent narcotic no different from anything you shoot up
your arm or snort up your nose. But it doesn't last. It takes
you up and it drops you down, hard, and coming off fame is
a slower, more painful process than cold turkey.

The morning after the Brighton show, the day of the last
gig at the Hammersmith Palais, I felt alone in the world,
naked, shaved hairless and wrapped in clingfilm, slopping in
a sea of piss and bumping up against the turds in the toilet
bowl at the end of the world. But it was meant to be the
biggest day of my life and this dichotomy made me angry.
And I grew thankful for that anger because it got me through
the morning, got me out of the toilet at Andrew's house
where I was doing my usual trick, but this time I had been
sitting, dressed but unshaven, unwashed throughout the
entire night, my brain still humming from the line of coke I
had on the tour bus back to London, smoking Marlboros
and ganja between coughing fits and staring at the wall.

Walls had been constant companions since Sheffield. I had studied the walls of Bath, Manchester and some of the other great cities of Britain. They were all the same, unsmiling, unhelpful, but Andrew's wall had gone through some amazing transformations. It had begun as a sheet of white, a blank canvas, slowly the lead characters in this lunatic's play I was living through had danced on to the backdrop, Jan and John in all the positions of the *Kama Sutra* and some the editors felt inappropriate. There was Tom and Alannah, the beautiful girlfriend of the band's agent, Joe quoting Shakespeare. But gradually they had all grown tired and gone to sleep, leaving the wall to froth and ferment. And out of it grew demons and devils who opened the curtain to a gaping chasm, a black hole that was sucking me in, pulling me towards it down into the abyss.

But then, I discovered, you can have too much self-pity, you can have too much self-laceration, and so finally the anger came. I thought of all that had got me here, all the long hours, the painful weeks, the months, the years of hard work, all the energy, the risks I had taken and the sacrifices I had made. I remembered rehearsal rooms and lyric sheets, overdrafts and grant cheques, the coiled lead of my efforts, struggling along Southend High Street on a Sunday morning with an amp so heavy I thought my arms would break, the apathy of record executives, the stone-cold, rock-hard gigs with an audience of seven. And then . . . the triumph of making it. I was fucked if Jan was going to ruin it all.

And so I appeared as a different person when I arrived at Tom and Alannah's ready for the cars to take us to the venue. The sound-check went smoothly and as long as I could ignore Jan's presence and pass John without a word, I felt fine. Then, after everything was prepared we still had two hours until the doors opened and another two before the gig. The last thing I could contemplate was to hang around the dressing room or anywhere near the others, and so I took myself off into the wet streets of London. Soon I found myself in a payphone, where I called my friend Helen, then in her second year at Oxford and whom I'd last seen at the house-freezing party. I asked her if she would like to come to the show that night.

Weeks earlier, during rehearsals, I had been given a guest list and asked who I would like to add to it for the last night at the Hammersmith Palais. I had put down the names of my parents, my elder brother and his family, school friends and college drinking partners and former neighbours and my family's neighbours. And to my amazement, they had all accepted the invitation, they were all there.

I didn't see any of them before the show. From seven o'clock onwards, none of us were allowed to leave the backstage area. There was a suite of rooms, but it was crowded with road crew, record executives coming to see the showcase gig, agents, publicists and a small group of journalists who had been granted an interview. It felt horribly claustrophobic. I just wanted to get out there and play the songs. I think even then a part of me knew this would be the last time I would play with the band.

And, when the hours had finally passed, Tears for Fears had played and our time came, it was a wonderful gig. But, walking from the stage, waving to the thousands in the audience, I felt like I was waving goodbye to my dreams.

Immediately after the show it seemed there was no contact between any of us. Tom was backstage with a journalist, I lost sight of Alannah and Joe, John was nowhere to be seen and Jan had gone off somewhere. I changed quickly into a pair of baggy black trousers and a grey grandpa vest and went into the thinning audience to see people as the disco played 'Come On Eileen', but I was really only looking for one person.

A few moments later I found my mum and dad and young

sister, Kim, looking lost and overwhelmed in a sea of post-punk teendom. Kim was the right age to enjoy it, but my parents didn't really know what to do or say; but who could have blamed them? This was Culture-shock Central. The last time they had seen me play was in the local church hall in Southend with two spotlights and a stylophone. We smiled and tried to speak to each other over the noise, but couldn't hear a word even when we yelled in each other's ears, so it was out to the bar and my father patting me on the back (something he had never done before), and my mother looking more anxious than usual. It was all clear. They knew.

'We saw Janet,' my mother said and then took a sip of her gin and tonic. My father avoided my gaze. 'I'm sorry, Mike,' he said quietly, and with an exchange of looks made familiar by years of living under the same roof and the little matter of a few genes, nothing more was said and we all silently agreed to let the matter pass.

And with it went what I thought at that moment would be my final contact with my mother and father. I thought I would pass for ever from their line of vision, disappear. I remember thinking Jan had been the one point of contact between them and me through recent years, and all the tricycles, holidays in Yarmouth and happy snaps with me, my dad and an end-of-pier monkey counted for too little when it came to understanding how I connected with the world. I sensed then that they could not and would not come any further into this universe of mine; coming to the show had been enough. I couldn't have expected more, they had already put up with the arrogant cuckoo I had become, they had lost the son they had wanted to become a scientist or a doctor and Jan had been the soft focus to counter my steely ambition, an ambition that had made me discard anything in my path I mistakenly thought superfluous.

I knew my parents were proud of me and affectionate, but we had run out of words and rather than regress to grunts and hand signals we chose to keep to our respective tribes. Their youth had been Glenn Miller and Sid Lawrence, mine Glen Matlock and Syd Barrett. We moved in different worlds like ghosts existing in parallel universes, in the same room but invisible. I was amazed they had recognised me at all. There I was, spiky red hair and a pony-tail, ten pounds lighter, the tramp-chic ragamuffin image taken to an extreme.

I left them with kisses and promises to write as soon as I got to the States, turned out of the bar, and there she was. And for a moment I thought she was the most beautiful woman in the world.

Helen and I had known one another for two years. Our first meeting was memorable not because of anything we did or said but because of something that had just happened the other side of the world. We were slotting letters into pigeon-holes in the Southend sorting office and had been drawn into an argument with a pair of octogenarian retired postmen about The Beatles, whom they had hated. The argument left unresolved, our break had come around and Helen and I had gone off to the canteen for tea and a sticky bun. Ten minutes later we returned to the pigeonholes and the same octoge-narians told us gleefully that John Lennon had been shot dead in New York.

Helen was a Fine Arts student at Jesus College, Oxford, and I think we fancied each other from the start. But even though Jan was then beginning her string of odd relation-ships, I must have been tuned out because I never made a move towards Helen, although her six-foot-six rugby-playing boyfriend may have had some influence on my thinking. But we had grown close. I used to go to see her at her parents' house during the summer. We drank tea in her studio and talked. She introduced me to the work of Egon Schiele and Klimt, and taught me to loathe Monet. We swapped books, she gave me Aldous Huxley's *The Doors of*

Perception and I got her into Henry Miller, I introduced her to Tangerine Dream and Stockhausen and she encouraged me to buy a Satie collection. We harboured a fantasy that one of us could acquire some Mescal and spend an afternoon experimenting with it, but we never did. In long letters we offered one another our philosophies and dreams, and that was it. Even when she asked a second time if I would be interested in modelling for her in her studio, the penny still didn't drop.

And when we met again that night I wanted to just leave the Hammersmith Palais and have done with it, but of course I couldn't, and with Helen I suddenly felt alive again after days in a catatonic state. There was an end-of-tour party and I guided Helen through the hubbub and then the security checks to the backstage area.

The dressing rooms were even more crowded than before the gig. I caught sight of Jan in one corner talking to John, both of them earnest and intense about something. Tom spotted us and fought his way over. I introduced Helen and he made a great show of kissing her hand and asking her how she knew me, and as she was talking Tom caught my eye and gave me one of his all-embracing smiles. For the moment at least everything felt just fine.

Two hours later I said goodbye to Tom, I couldn't see the others, and as Helen turned to leave he touched my shoulder and said quietly, 'Let's talk . . . tomorrow.' A car took us to Andrew's house in Clapham. The place was empty. I made tea and Helen and I sat on the floor as we once had in her studio, centuries in the past. Neither of us slept that night, we had too much to talk about.

Wednesday 3 November was freezing but the sky was the purest, freshest blue. As the band had performed the previous night, a new TV station, Channel 4, had started transmitting. In Poland, Lech Walesa was unaware that he would be freed within a week and Leonid Brezhnev was entering the final few days of his life. London was soon to fade behind me in the jetstream, at least that had been the plan. Now I wasn't so sure. Could I stomach a world tour after what had happened?

Helen was a salve, a stabiliser, the perfect remedy and I had absolutely nothing planned. For the first time in months I could do exactly what I liked. We took the tube into the centre of London and just walked, walked and talked – should I stay or should I go? We had lunch on our laps by the river sitting on the wall near the Tate, sharing the thud of traffic with the lapping brown Thames to our backs. And in the Tate, standing before Millais's *Christ in the House of His Parents*, I suddenly knew what choices to make. It was nothing to do with God or any crap like that, it was the godlike part of Millais that had touched me. Suddenly, pop music, careers, adoring audiences and even the prospect of touring the world seemed insignificant. I looked at the face of Christ and the faces of Mary and Joseph, at the wood-shavings, the blood on the boy's palms, the marks in flesh, the knowing look. I had more important things to do, I convinced myself.

It was only later that I knew the thought of over-hearing Jan and John shagging in the next room in some Chicago hotel may also have been a crucial factor in the decision-making process.

22

Tom's hair looked very red in the light coming from the kitchen, and the hands in which he had just cupped his face appeared abnormally white. For the first time I noticed how much his tan had faded. He looked up and I could see he hadn't slept much either.

We were in his sitting room, alone in the house. Across the street, Jan and John were in bed, it was early evening, the sun gone, frost on the windows. I had just told him I had to leave the band.

'And you're sure that's what you want?' he said, looking at me intently.

I felt curiously numb, the hysteria had passed and I could meet his eye with a strange new self-confidence.

'I've thought about nothing else all day and I can't really see myself on the coach with Janet and John, can you?' I said. 'I don't think it'll be like the kids' books.'

He gave a weak smile and then his expression changed. 'God, this is so fucking ridiculous!'

I said nothing, just looked at him. My own calm was beginning to unnerve me.

'I can help a bit,' he said softly, 'but things are . . .'

'Yeah, I know.'

'I can get you some money, what you would have earned in the States. It'll help.'

'That would be great,' I replied flatly.

He stood up and ran his hands through his hair. 'I'll talk to him tomorrow,' he said and nodded almost imperceptibly in the direction of the house across the street. 'But, what are you going to do, Mikey?'

I stood up. 'To be honest, Tom, I don't have a fucking clue. Fun, isn't it?' We walked to the door. 'Well, I say I haven't a clue. I'm going to talk to Jan, tonight if I can, and then I need to get out of London. But after that . . .'

I stood on the freezing path. Tom was shivering in the doorway. I made an attempt to smile. 'Well, what can I say? Good luck is I think, quite unnecessary.'

Tom took a step on to the path and hugged me. 'I'm so sorry this has happened,' he said gently.

'Look, it's nothing to do . . . Just, well, let's try to keep in touch, yeah?'

He stepped into the doorway and I turned and walked to the street without looking back.

For a few moments I didn't quite know what to do. I sat on the curb outside Tom and Alannah's and looked up at the windows of John's place. Frost lay crisp and fresh on the road. I wrapped my greatcoat around me, walked over, knocked on John's door and waited.

A few moments later Jan answered the door. She was dressed in a robe, her hair a mess. She looked startled to see me, then gave me a weak smile.

'I wondered if we could talk,' I said and gave her a look

that said: 'You must do this one last thing for me.'

For a second she hesitated, looked back along the hall, then said. 'Give me two minutes.'

We walked in silence along Lillieshall Road and a few minutes later found ourselves on the edge of Clapham Common, our breath visible in the air, the cold seeping through to my bones.

Of course I wanted to ask what everyone asks, I wanted to hurt myself with her responses, and like everyone else, I did ask. There are no answers to those questions other than ones that pierce and freeze the heart; I knew that then, everyone has always known it, but we still ask. Then, after the mania, the wounds still bleeding and wet, I told her I could not go on with the tour. She wasn't at all surprised, just relieved.

For some reason I expected a little remorse, a little regret, but there was none, Jan was far too excited, far too wrapped up in herself and her new man. She didn't want to hurt me any more than I was already hurt, but equally she could offer me nothing. Somehow I had delivered her into a life of fulfilment. Now, I thought, she had the lot. I suppose I should have felt angry, but it was almost as though her happiness was a little too much, a little too intense to be real. She now seemed to be the one on the edge of hysteria. Even then I must have sensed something dark coming up fast on the outside track, something that was about to smack into her very, very hard.

Across the dark Common with the stars defeating the street lights, our years together dropped from her like water from an oil-drenched bird, and magically, they clung to me, adding to my own memories, multiplying my own regrets, my own mistakes.

Back on the corner of Lillieshall Road we stood and looked each other in the face for the last time. It was a moment in sharp focus, crystal clear, even then etching itself into my

mind. Reaching into her pocket, Jan pulled out her engage-
ment ring, an unofficial symbol we had shared a couple of
years earlier. She held it between us, and I took it numbly. I
kissed her on the cheek and she giggled, pulling away
abruptly, as though it was an act of adultery. Running, she
returned to John's house and I watched her until she turned
on to the path and out of view.

34

The Vauxhall Viva was parked outside Andrew's house. Inside it was almost everything I owned – a few clothes, a cheap stereo, a box of records, two boxes of books, a type-writer, my guitar and amp, a scrapbook filled with Watch With Mother and Colour-Me-Pop memorabilia and a metal box crammed full with tapes of my songs.

For a long time I sat in the driver's seat turning over Jan's ring in my pocket, my mind so flooded with thoughts I could not focus on any one of them. I pulled out the ring and looked at it. A solitaire I had bought her from a market stall in Devon one summer. It had cost almost nothing, but then I had nothing, so that had been okay.

I stared through the windscreen, the cars passing by heading for the main road and I thought of The Beatles' long and winding road and of Tolkien's comment that from your doorstep a single road leads everywhere. But which road was

I to take? I really did have no idea. One: I could not go back to Southend or anywhere near there. Two: I did not want to stay in London. Three: I wanted to be with young people, people I thought were like me, people I should have been with all along.

Bizarrely, I remembered my sixth form and sitting in the special class for Oxbridge candidates. I was six weeks through the process with a place organised for me at Cambridge. At the break my form teacher asked me to stay behind. He had a copy of my application form before him on the desk. 'Michael,' he said, a little concerned. 'You haven't put your French O-level down here.' I had looked at him, confused. 'I don't have French O-level,' I replied.

That had been the end of my Oxbridge hopes; O-level French was mandatory for Oxbridge entrance. I had been one of the school's most promising entrants, now they were not happy with me. It was the end of my 'academic period' – the second year of the sixth form became a blur, guitars became more important than Boyle's gas laws, the *NME* was read more thoroughly than my course books. I did nothing but rehearse and listen to Yes, and ended up almost failing my A-levels. Now, of all moments, for some inexplicable reason, I knew I wanted to try to turn back the clock, to make amends, for myself, if no one else.

But where was it to be? Oxford or Cambridge? I tried to weigh everything up. As a kid I had been heading for Cambridge, I had liked it there the day I visited for an interview, but from here in Clapham Cambridge was much further than Oxford – would the car make it? Oxford was also beautiful and of course Helen was there. I decided to toss a coin; heads Oxford, tails Cambridge. I watched it flip over in the air catching the yellow from the street lights, then it was nestled into my palm, I turned it on to the back of my hand and there was the Queen; Oxford it was.

The stereo didn't work, I had five pounds seventeen pence

in my pocket, just enough petrol to reach Oxford, a credit card at its limit (a chirpy £250), no food, just a bottle of water. I kept on my greatcoat because the heater had joined the stereo in its dotage, but even then my Chinese slippers offered a wafer-thin protection against the cold so my feet were freezing. All I possessed lay on the back seat of the car. I felt like a snail carrying its home around on its back.

Then the car began to act up. I had reached the point where the motorway passes by High Wycombe and hits a massive, grinding hill for about two miles. It was then the clutch decided to throw off the bandages the garage had applied, to chuck out the antibiotics and the pacemaker and take to its deathbed. The car slowed, and slowed some more. I shifted down and it slowed still further until I was crawling along the hard shoulder at 10 mph in first gear, praying I would make the peak of the hill so I could hit the relatively flat road that would take me to Oxford twenty miles on. And as the revs spluttered to almost nothing I made the peak of the hill and let the car roll down the other side on to the flat.

Thirty minutes later I was a few miles outside Oxford, but by now it was getting late, and I realised I couldn't go knocking on Helen's door. So I pulled into a lay-by at Forest Hill, just beyond the ring-road around Oxford, and sat in comforting darkness, the only light and the only sounds coming from the cars sweeping past.

I had never felt so alone. I took the ring from my pocket again. Devon, 1979, now seemed a very remote reality, someone else's perhaps.

I slept in snatches in the driver's seat, awakened by speeding lorries and later the rain falling torrentially on the roof of the car. Much later I watched the sun rising sore over the fields. By six, I could wait no longer and drove into Oxford. Of course, nothing was open. The streets of East Oxford, where every other house is a student hovel, were wet with rain and empty. In a doorway a lager can clattered and a stray page from an old newspaper rolled along the pavement before sticking to a garden wall. At seven o'clock I found a newsagent that was open. I bought a packet of biscuits and sat in the car thinking about the band. They would be packing now. Soon they would be driven to Heathrow and a waiting jumbo.

I left it until eight o'clock before I knocked on Helen's door. She tried to be pleased to see me, but I hadn't told her I would be turning up in Oxford quite then. She came to the door in an over-sized rugby shirt – the boyfriend's. The body that normally filled it (rather less decoratively I might add) was upstairs in bed. But by this time I had little pride left. Helen invited me in for breakfast and I accepted, and when the boyfriend left for college an hour later, Helen and I sat by her open fire, logs burned comfortingly and we nursed cups of tea as I told her about my conversations with Tom and Jan. I thought again about where I should have been at that moment, checking in my guitar at Heathrow; but I told Helen that I was, in a sense, relieved. And I suppose I was. I told her I was going to stay in Oxford now, find a room, try to find some other part of myself, check out whether there was anything there.

The tea finished, Helen took a shower and I was alone in the large square sitting room of the house she shared with five other students. I listened to the creaking of the floorboards, the ubiquitous indefinable sounds of old houses, and over that, the sound of spray from the shower cubicle along the hall, Helen slopping the water against the glass walls, spray ricocheting from her body. Beyond these sounds I could hear the roar of take-off, the captain's announcements, the rattle of the overhead lockers. Isolated, the world a distant place, I threw myself on to the cushions beside me on the sofa and cried until the fabric was wet.

25

I could stay no more than a couple of days sleeping on the sofa at Helen's. I knew that if I was to get over things and start again, the first priority was to find a place of my own. By accepting what had happened I found the energy to get moving and then things began to fall into place fairly quickly. Helen found me a tiny attic room with sloping ceilings in a large corner house off Iffley Road. The rent was £25 a week inclusive of amenities.

True to his word, Tom had arranged to send me some money, a part at least of what I would have earned on the US leg of the tour. But I knew I would need more than cash to help rebuild my life and before leaving London I had arranged for a chunk of the money to come in the form of a four-track tape recorder upon which I could write and record solo material. This I saw as my lifeline to a new world, my way of getting back into the music business under my own terms. Tom had the money sent to one of my sisters, who then forwarded it to Helen's address in Oxford. It wasn't much, £300, but it meant I could recharge my credit card and put down two weeks' rent.

Two days after arriving at Helen's front door I took the Vauxhall Viva on what turned out to be its last journey across Oxford and transferred my worldly goods to the attic room. The next day I called the tape-recorder distributor Tom had told me about and they had my order ready for delivery. That afternoon I joined the millions on the register of unemployed and stood in a long queue in a beige-coloured, low-ceilinged room reading the showbiz page of the *Sun* over someone's shoulder. Later that day the car was sent for scrap, bolstering my funds by a handsome £10, and Helen escaped from the boyfriend for the evening and turned up with a house-warming present of a bottle of Moët.

Over the champagne we talked about what I was planning to do. I actually had no real plans, more a programme of intent, but it was something. I wasn't giving up, that was Statement One. I would scrape by on the dole, record some new material and use my new-found contacts to get a recording deal. I would then form a band, play gigs, record albums. One day I would be back at E-Z Hire and Rak Studios if I chose to be, and the Hammersmith Palais, or better still, the Odeon, Wembley, Madison Square Garden.

I can do this, I thought. The champagne helped of course, but that old self-protecting immunity to criticism was kicking in yet again. It seemed nothing could keep it down. Jan had gone, sure, and that still cut deep, but fuck her, I thought, I wrote the songs, I played most of the instruments and wrote most of the lyrics. I could find a singer, or do it myself. It would work this time.

I had one more errand to run before I could settle down to re-forging my career. When Jan and I moved to London to join the Twins we had left some of the old band's equipment at Jan's father's house in Southend. There were mics, stands, another amp, an acoustic guitar, some percussion, an echo machine, bits and pieces I would need for my new life. During our walk on Clapham Common Jan had told me to take anything I wanted. I decided to hire a car and collect the stuff. Jan's father did not own a telephone (after all, this was 1982), and so I would just have to turn up and hope for the best.

Naturally Southend had not changed a speck, but I could imagine I had been away for a century. I felt like an astronaut in the old relativity paradox, returning to earth after what to him was a five-year trip to find that all his friends and family had died fifty years earlier. But all the ghosts of my past were still here, behind their curtains, at their desks, playing in bars and rehearsing in garages. I just prayed I wouldn't bump into anyone I had once known.

But of course, I did. Dave Barker was a some-time member of various outfits I had been party to, he had shared a flat with my old friend Tim and knew absolutely everyone on the Southend music scene. A mile short of Jan's father's house I rather foolishly decided to stop at a garage in the centre of town to buy some chocolate, and as I returned to the car, Dave stepped out of his. He looked at me and then did a double-take. For a moment he seemed confused, but I could smell his excitement. He knew something was very wrong.

'Hello, Dave,' I said, and tried my best to look comfortable and confident.

'I could ask the obvious, couldn't I?' he replied.

I looked at the oil-stained tarmac, at the dirty hem of my greatcoat and the weathered Chinese slippers. I decided there was no escape. I could only retreat into honesty.

'Jan and I have split up,' I announced. It was the first time I had actually said it, and I felt a lump growing huge in my throat. I stared straight at him. 'She fell in love with the Twins' manager. They left for New York two days ago. I'm on the dole, in Oxford.' My eyes were watering, but there was nothing I could do about it.

Dave, who I never really liked that much, was speechless for a moment. You could read the rapidly shifting emotions in his face, and then, to my amazement, he clasped my shoulders and said with genuine warmth, 'God, Mike, I'm really sorry.'

I could find few words after that. We each mumbled something about keeping in touch, meeting up for a beer, each knowing we would almost certainly do nothing about it, each for different reasons, wanting to get away as quickly as possible. I drove off, pride holding back the bitterness until I had turned the corner out of sight.

Jan's old street was almost silent. I prayed her father would be in. I just wanted to get my stuff and go. Already Oxford felt like home. I parked, marched to the front door and rang the bell. There was no reply. I rang again, still no reply. I remembered how deaf her father was and rapped the heavy brass knocker and leaned on the bell. Finally, I could see a moving shape blurred by the semi-opaque glass of the door. A moment later, Jan's father was there, his hands smeared with mud from his garden, a streak of soil across his cheek. For a second I thought he didn't recognise me, then his face relaxed. 'Hello,' he mumbled.

'Hello,' I replied. 'I've come to pick up a few things. Did Jan say anything?'

His face was expressionless. He stepped to one side and beckoned me into the hall. It smelled of damp, and immediately the memories flooded in. I was about to take a step along the hall but he suddenly gripped my elbow. I turned and could see his face in the dim light from the door. It was only then I noticed how much he had aged since I had seen him last.

He made to speak, but stopped. Then he tried again. 'Jan,' he said so quietly I could hardly make out the word. And suddenly I knew something terrible had happened. It felt as though every muscle in my body tightened at precisely the same moment.

'Jan,' he said again, a little louder. 'Jan has had a nervous breakdown . . . in New York.'

36

Blaise Pascal once suggested the idea that we all have a 'pyramid of dependency'. People can't think about luxuries or be creative unless the foundations are there – food, shelter, rest. And the reverse is also true: as we face successively bigger problems we turn to more and more fundamental resources in order to cope. Because of this, my first thought was that I wanted to speak to my father.

After all I had concluded about my relationship with my parents, I now knew that they were the only people in the world I wanted to see at that moment. I needed to find home, find Mum and Dad.

The journey to my parents' house in darkest Essex was a meaningless backdrop to my thoughts; emotions jostled for priority. I was angry that she hadn't just faded away into my past, angry, believing that John had let her down. Part of me was pleased: 'See how it all goes wrong without me?'

Another part was puzzled; had she realised she really did love me and not John, and the strain had become too much? But above all, I saw myself in the role of the white knight who would ride off to the citadel and rescue the distressed maiden; a late-twentieth-century version in which the white knight had red spiky hair and the maiden was in a New York nut-house . . . all very post-modern.

My parents still lived in the house on the council estate my elder sister had found them five years earlier. I had visited only two or three times during that five years and I couldn't bear the place. It was a brick box dumped along with a few others in the middle of a muddy field. My father no longer had the energy to decorate it properly and it was sparsely furnished with pieces that had found their way to the back storeroom of charity shops. I knew I was an ungrateful little bastard for never going there and the guilt kept me away more than the grim swirly carpets and blank walls.

My mother opened the door and simply stared at me in disbelief, but after the shock had passed she and my father sat me down and gave me tea and offered me biscuits, and for a moment allowed fresh guilt to melt away some of the other pain.

I told them what had happened and they listened in silence, growing more and more distressed by the news. They had suffered more than their fair share of misery during their lives. My mother had had a series of nervous breakdowns during the 1950s and undergone brutal electro-therapy. She had never been the same after that, but, more than anyone, she must have known what Jan was going through. My father's first wife and baby had died during childbirth in 1939, something I had only learned from my sister two years earlier, something he had never told me. So, with that trauma and my mother's illness, Dad knew what I was feeling. In fact, between them they knew everything.

On the journey there I had formulated something of a

plan, and I told my parents what I was going to do. I would contact the hotel in Manhattan and try to speak to John and then I would get the first available flight out. I'd call the bank and get an overdraft to pay for it. My parents just nodded, although my mother looked concerned. Majorca had been the limit of their world – ships fell over the edge beyond Formentera.

And after half an hour I told them I had to go. They asked if I would like to stay the night, but knew I couldn't. I kissed my mother goodbye and she went into the kitchen. My father led me along the hall to the front door. Then, as I shook his hand, he shocked me by throwing his arms around me and pulling me to him, holding me tight to his chest. It was only then as I felt his back and his shoulders I realised just how thin he had become. His cheeks were sagging, his eyes contained all his life's pain, agonies that made me feel like a baby in his arms once more. And at that moment, I wished I was.

I said goodbye and was turning to the door when my father said: 'Mike, I know this isn't much, but it might help.' I looked at his hands. He was removing a cheap digital watch from his wrist and handing it to me.

'No Dad, really.'

But he was pushing it towards me.

'No, it's okay,' I muttered.

Then I looked into his eyes again. He needed to give me this; it was all he had.

I took it and hugged him again; his wet cheek on mine.

37

Mid-flight, the face that stared back at me from the mirror in the cabin toilet was surely not mine. I looked ten years older. But by now I was running on pure, high-octane adrenaline and an over-riding, naïve belief that I could do something, change things, make everything better.

The journey from JFK to midtown Manhattan would one day become familiar, a fifteen-mile stretch that would, during later visits to the city, pass as a blank, but that first time, I was alive to everything and felt as though I had touched down on an alien world. The Van Wyck Expressway swept me north past Shea Stadium, skirting La Guardia airport and took me on to my first view of Manhattan: there, piercing the clouds, the Twin Towers and along the horizon, the Empire State Building.

The cab driver was so stoned I'm sure the car was driving itself, at least I hoped it was. As we swerved into an available car-sized gap in the traffic, the Hendrix track on the radio cut suddenly to a DJ reporting that a man was at that moment suspended from the Brooklyn Bridge in a harness. He had a bag filled with grenades and was threatening to throw them in the river 'to kill the pollution'. The cab driver turned to me, a big white grin slashing his ebony face. 'Welcome to New York City, my man,' he slurred.

New York in 1982 was a very different city from New York today, and was probably at its lowest ebb. Times Square was a seedy mish-mash of porn emporia, peep shows and strip clubs. There were tramps everywhere, they sat bedraggled and bone-thin on every street corner and lined the outside of Chase Manhattan Bank on Fifth Avenue. Most of Central Park was a no-go zone and only locals or those tired of living ventured north of 96th Street unless they had to.

I was shocked. New York impressed me, of course, how could it not? But apart from the architecture it was nothing like I had imagined it. In my dreams it was a city out of *Metropolis*, but in Technicolor, huge, staggeringly wealthy, chic. To an English kid growing up in 1960s Britain, all Americans were rich. I had seen *I Love Lucy*, I knew; even the Flintstones had been a two-car family. But seeing the tramps and the dented, rusting gas-guzzlers, the crumbling bridges, the pot-holed roads and leaking drains, all my illusions were shattered. It was a cartoon city but daubed in ochre and blood red.

The Twins were staying at the Iroquois on 44th Street. On a recent visit to New York I discovered it is now one of the 'Leading Hotels of the World', but in 1982 it was the worst flea-pit this side of Calcutta. Cockroaches outnumbered the guests a thousand to one, and room service came in the form of ten-dollar hookers moonlighting from their regular jobs on 42nd Street two blocks down. It was very rock 'n' roll.

I arrived at six in the evening to find the only person from the Twins' entourage still staying there was John. The others had left that morning for their first date the following night at a club in Trenton, about thirty miles away. John was out but had left a note detailing how to get to the hospital and a promise to see me before I left.

By the time I checked in and washed my face it was dark, the view from my window a fractured neon mosaic. I had been told to look as poor as possible and never to carry more than ten dollars on me, so in the lobby I left my wallet (for what it was worth) with a receptionist, then asked her how to get to 183rd Street. She looked at me in disbelief. I told her I had to see someone at St Luke's and her features softened. She was black, very pretty and now, suddenly, exquisitely motherly.

Carla lived on 98th and said her train would take me on to 182nd Street station, and that I could get a bus directly outside that would take me to the hospital. The journey seemed interminable, it was freezing and at each stop a blast of cold, filthy air gushed into the compartment. In this subterranean world, the slashed seats and the train windows blanked out completely by meaningless graffiti and grime, I could feel an energy, malevolent and volatile.

And soon, after two blocks on a bus on the evening route from 'Purgatory Westside' to 'Hell Central', I stepped down to the road outside the gates of St Luke's Psychiatric Hospital, a huge grey slab set down in the centre of the urban killing fields.

'Jan is in there,' I thought. 'Jan, who only a few months ago sat with me eating a Chinese take-away and watching *Mork and Mindy* on TV, Jan who had said I looked like a guitarist, Jan, who started it all, who had always been there.'

But then, later, after seeing her as though through a Perspex divide, as though she had been frozen in a different time and left nothing but an afterglow in this world, it was obvious I had wasted my time. I could no longer reach her, my white stallion trotted off, my armour crumbled at my feet.

I walked along the corridor. I wasn't sure what to do next. For a strange moment I felt calm, I believed I could feel no more, I had reached the point of emotional overload. Then I heard someone call me; looking up from the floor and the reflections of the overhead lights, I saw John striding towards me.

We drove almost the length of Manhattan. He seemed calm, but I knew he was suppressing his own panic – John was the sort of person who buried anxiety with responsibility. I felt like a child and he knew it. I was grateful he had turned up but I was not so naïve as to think he had done it as a favour. I had walked away from the Twins, and he wanted to prove he was still very much in control. And of course he was. What had I been thinking, rushing into this scene, trying to prise open the slammed shut door that led to the world I had been part of a few days earlier? They lived in a parallel universe now and had left me behind.

John bought me supper, we walked through the Village, we had a beer, we talked about Jan. And finally I learned what had happened.

It had been the band's first day in New York. John and Jan had gone shopping in the Village. They'd had a pizza just off Washington Square. Jan seemed fixated with the Twin Towers a dozen or so blocks downtown and had kept saying she wanted to go there and 'lean out into the wind'. He thought she was behaving a little oddly, but had put it down to excitement; the band's first US dates were not far off.

John had the room next to hers at the hotel and about ten in the evening he heard, coming through the wall, the sound of crashing. He had tried to ignore it, but it had grown steadily worse. The TV went on full-blast, then he heard the bathroom door slam several times, a continuous flushing of the cistern, followed by a loud bang. A few minutes later he knocked on her door to see if she was okay, but there had been no reply. The next thing he knew one of the road crew was rushing down the stairs calling him. Jan was up on the roof.

As he emerged on to the roof he saw Jan running towards the parapet. Then she stopped abruptly and turned. She had painted herself red. She was wearing a red dress, her hair had been dyed crimson and her face, hands, arms and legs were painted flame red. Her eyes looked wild and unfocused. Behind her had lain the panorama of New York, the Chrysler Building lit up and glorious. But he was not really taking it in, just watching Jan move slowly to the edge of the roof. He remembered how cold it had been up there.

Then he heard a noise from behind him. He span round and Tom and Chris Turner, the road manager, were emerging from the roof exit. He didn't know how they had got there but he was relieved to see them.

Jan had inched further towards the parapet of the building and had taken a step up on to the concrete sill. John had edged towards her slowly. She seemed to grow calmer when she saw him. He had gently asked her what she was doing. She hadn't replied, just took a step towards him. Then as she had reached him, her fist had flown at his face and caught him on the jaw. She had laughed hysterically and spun round again, but before she could take a step, John had grabbed her arm. His hand slipped on her sweat and the running paint and she started to writhe and scream uncontrollably.

'We called an ambulance,' John said slowly, looking away. 'They took her straight to St Luke's.'

I had listened in silence and now I felt slightly nauseous. Clearly, Jan was gone from John's life too. He, the band, the 'organisation' would help her in every way they could, they would try to get her home, she was insured, she would be safe, but John had disengaged. He had had to.

And for a moment I wondered if I could not turn back the clock, ask everyone to forget what had happened and let me join the US leg of the tour after all. But that could never have happened; they had all now disengaged from me *and* Jan. I was as much a part of the parcel as her. The door to their world was not just closed, it had been locked and securely bolted, from the inside.

38

Two days after visiting Southend, I was back in Oxford, and nothing had changed. Walking back along The High I looked at the faces of those who passed me and they knew nothing of what I had seen, what I had just done – how could they? For a while there I had hung out in an entirely different world; now I was back.

The winter of 1982 was the coldest and bleakest I could remember. I saw thick ice on the Cherwell, the gargoyles bedecked with snow, and I knew I had not left my problems behind in America, yet soon I began to love this city; Oxford seeped into my soul.

The social services were on strike throughout the winter of 1982 and even though I had to queue in the snow outside a disused school in the centre of Oxford each Wednesday morning to sign on, I only received £13 per week emergency payment and my rent was £25. Luckily I had an understanding landlord who knew the money would come through eventually and so I kept the £13 all to myself.

Even as a student I had never known such poverty. Literally every penny counted. I lived on baked beans, bananas and muesli bought from a store in East Oxford called Uhuru, which stood next door to the alternative bookshop, Mother Earth: full circle . . . how wonderful. I didn't drink or smoke and the days when cocaine would be placed before my nose (a single line costing what I had to live on for two weeks) were consigned to history.

I stayed at home all day keeping warm and writing page after page of a novel in the German Expressionist style, but what distinguished this from my efforts as a bored eighteen-year-old was that now I actually had some interesting experiences to draw upon. Each evening I would walk into the centre of Oxford. I wore eye make-up and the layered tramp look that hadn't quite yet hit the university, but soon would. On my head I wore a beret pushed back so that it perched at a ridiculous angle and displayed my long red Thompson Twin fringe; and, of course, on my freezing feet, the obligatory Chinese slippers. Crossing Magdalen Bridge I would be stopped at least once a night by Japanese tourists wanting to stand beside 'a punk' while their friends took pictures.

Although I felt utterly miserable, it was actually one of the most exciting periods of my life, a time during which I learned a great deal about myself and other people. Through Helen I was introduced to a large group of students and made many friends. I started to play in clubs, just jamming and having fun. Gradually word spread that a former Thompson Twin was living in Oxford and the party invites began to gather pace.

At student parties I would sometimes be treated like a visiting Punch and Judy show. I remember a party hosted by one of the Von Bismarcks at which a couple of brainless society gals thought I was 'really cute'. I wanted to vomit over them. At other more down-to-earth affairs female students miraculously turned into highly educated groupies who wanted to shag a 'pop star', and even an ex-'pop star' would do. But not everyone was phoney. I made some great friends, people I am still close to today. And eventually I started to slide back into music. I formed a new band called Colour-Me-Pop and we began rehearsing in an old barn out in the country to the west of Oxford.

I heard very little from New York. John Hade had paid for a friend of his who had trained as a psychologist to fly out to try to help Jan. I spoke to him a couple of times, but for the rest of 1982 at least, there was little change.

By the following spring the Thompson Twins were a household name. They were in the Top 5 with 'Love On Your Side' and every store, every office, everywhere it seemed, now bounced to the beat I had heard half-mixed at Rak and to which I had performed night after night only a few months earlier. People who knew me wondered how I felt about it, how I managed to deal with the weird dichotomy I was facing. I said then what I think now: 'There's nothing I can do about it.'

Then, in January 1983, Jan came home to England, and was admitted to a psychiatric hospital in Essex.

One particularly bitter morning a week later, I caught the first of four buses that would get me from Oxford to the hospital some eighty miles away. I don't remember what I expected to find, but to me Jan seemed no better. She was thinner, paler. There was a horrid, musty smell about her, which, I discovered later, came as a result of the cocktail of pharmaceuticals sloshing around her system. She looked at me with that same blank expression I had seen in New York. We sat for a while on a sofa in a recreational area. All around me were sick people. Some were staring at a black and white TV perched in a corner, others shuffled around aimlessly, some just sat silently staring into space waiting for their lives to end, for the world to pass away.

I felt incredibly uncomfortable, but the shock I had experienced in New York was no longer there. For months now I had lived with the knowledge that Jan had gone, I was almost used to the notion. This time I felt no desperate need to make her better, to find the healing touch.

So we sat. I held her hand. It felt clammy and I could feel each tiny bone. I smiled at her and I was surprised when she gave a faint smile back. I was telling her about all the things I'd been doing since November. I told her about Oxford, about the new band I was putting together, the new songs I'd written on the four-track and how I would like her to do some backing vocals when she was well again. Then suddenly, she turned to me and said, 'Tea.'

I looked at her, confused. And, like a two-year-old learning to speak, she said, 'You, tea?'

I just nodded. She got up from the sofa and one of the orderlies led her to another room and a few minutes later escorted her back with a cup of tea in her hand. He looked at me and indicated I should take it from her. But then, just as I reached for it, Jan threw the tea, the cup and the saucer on the floor at my feet. The saucer bounced and landed near the feet of an unblinking inmate, the cup shattered into a dozen pieces.

Jan howled with laughter and looked at my face, blanched with horror, and roared some more. 'Australia,' she said, pointing at the puddle of steaming tea. 'Australia.' And, looking at it, I could sort of see what she meant.

At first I really believed I could save Jan. I thought she would get well and come back to me and we could start over again. We could re-form the band and this time with the contacts we had made we would really make it big. But gradually I realised this would never happen and soon I didn't even want it to happen, but by then I had made for myself what passed for a life in Oxford. Before long I was starting on what I hoped would be the climb back to fame, success and hit singles, on my own.

Of course it didn't work, and to be fair, I had had my chance and for whatever reason, I had blown it. Maybe it had been my fault all along. Perhaps I possessed a self-destructive streak and had brought failure upon myself. Some might say I should have known joining the Twins was never going to work because the foundations had been rotten, my relationship with Jan had been a time-bomb ticking away in the background, and as we rehearsed and performed and the world seemed to finally click into a neat jigsaw, the bomb had gone off.

But for a while I sincerely believed that being an ex-Thompson Twin, however fleetingly, would get me back there. However, the harsh truth, especially in the brainless world of pop, is that nobody wants a loser and nobody trusts a musician who some might have perceived as a destructive influence. I knew I had been the innocent party but not everyone shared that view. Yet even that could have been overcome, there have been bigger problems in other people's lives. The simple truth is that I just didn't have what it takes, I didn't have every element in place and so I became an also-ran.

Years of struggle, barrels of self-confidence and optimism, hopes, dreams and determination are hard to break down and all the logic, the arguments, the obvious, glaring facts of failure still do not stop people trying to succeed. For three more years I kept going, I kept fighting. I had lost a career, lost a girlfriend, let this ogre dominate my entire life, but still I kept on. And in the end, it was nothing obvious that made me stop and change for ever the direction in which I was racing. It was something simple, something that burst out from inside. Late in 1984, at the height of their fame, the

Thompson Twins played at the Apollo Theatre in Oxford, and quite out of the blue the promoters called me and asked if I would like to be put on the guest-list.

I was staggered by the show, bowled over by the changes; the Thompson Twins were now truly world-class. I sat in the audience watching the pyrotechnics, hearing the screaming children who made up most of the audience and I checked myself. I should be feeling something, I thought, anything. Surely, I should be incandescent with envy and frustration. But actually, when I dug deep to find a reaction at all, it was, well, *embarrassment*, and a strange sadness. The Twins were very rich, they were at their absolute peak, they were famous, they had everything; by comparison, I had nothing. But then I looked at the faces of the crowd, those young faces, too young, too eager, and I felt embarrassed for Tom, for Joe, even for Alannah. The Thompson Twins were teeny-stars.

These little boys and girls in the audience were not the fans I had been so inspired by on the tour. Some of them were with their mums and dads, for God's sake! In that moment I knew this road I had travelled along had to be a dead-end. Nothing that had happened to me in almost a decade of struggle affected me so dramatically as that realisation. I suddenly knew that even if, through all adversity, you clung on and dragged yourself through and 'got there', 'there' was not such a great place after all. 'There' was populated with pre-pubescents, tacky T-shirts and over-priced programmes, screaming children who cared nothing for what you had poured into your music, children who would dump you as soon as another newer, shinier model came along.

Even then this feeling may not have lasted. Surely, I would simply return home, pick up my guitar and feel insulated from the experience at the Apollo and that all-embracing self-motivation would return. But this time it didn't go, this time the disillusionment stayed with me.

And gradually, I began to conceive the unthinkable. I

could, I realised, just walk away from it all. There was no shame in failure. In fact, it took a kind of courage to leave behind something you had dedicated your life to but knew was wrong for you, to let it go.

Some may say only cowards give up, but insisting that something is right when it is patently wrong takes much more than cowardice, it requires stupidity. And I had had quite enough of being stupid.

POSTSCRIPT

The Thompson Twins went from strength to strength. They appeared at Live Aid in Philadelphia and Madonna came on to duet with Tom for one song. Between 1982 and 1989 they sold an estimated 25 million records. But soon after I saw them in Oxford, the edifice began to crumble. Joe Leeway left the band in 1986 and their 1987 album, *Close to the Bone*, received a muted reception. From then on the hits dried up and Tom turned to writing for other artists. A few months later, the Thompson Twins split acrimoniously with John Hade. Today, Tom and Alannah live in New Zealand and record under the moniker Babble, and Joe lives in Los Angeles, where he has a recording studio.

Jan recovered from her problems and left hospital in 1983. I stayed in touch with her for a couple of years; she came to a few early Colour-Me-Pop gigs, which was weird to say the least. I lost touch with her in 1985 but have been told she became a teacher, and that she married and has children.

I really did give up music and eventually succeeded as an author, but I have yet to publish a novel written in the style of the German Expressionists.